A GUIDE TO HASSIDISM

A GUIDE TO
HASSIDISM

by

Rabbi Dr. H. Rabinowicz, b.a., ph.d.

NEW YORK   THOMAS YOSELOFF   LONDON

Prepared under the editorial direction of
the World Jewish Congress: British Section
and published by
Thomas Yoseloff: London and New York

Printed in Great Britain
by Charles Birchall & Sons, Ltd.
Liverpool and London

Dedicated to
the Sacred Memory of my Father
Rabbi Nathan David Rabinowicz
of Biala

CONTENTS

PREFACE

HASSIDISM is the story of a great religious revivalist movement which was born in Eastern Europe in the middle of the eighteenth century. Hassidism came into being in a dark age of spiritual sterility and physical persecution. And to the humble people of Israel it brought a new message of hope and consolation. With precepts sublimely simple, Hassidism stressed the cardinal virtues that the prophets preached and raised the man in the market place to the spiritual level of the *Talmid Haham*.

Great men arose in Israel, *Zaddikim*, who lead the people wisely and well in the paths of the Torah, who helped them to live full and satisfying lives on earth and to reach for Heaven. In the past two centuries, Jewry has produced more outstanding leaders than in any other period since the days of the *Tannaim* and *Amoraim* of the talmudic epoch.

Hassidic philosophy has given a new dimension to day-to-day life, and some two thousand works of Hassidic literature have enriched the minds of men. Hassidic bibliography still awaits its Steinschneider. Only an encyclopaedia could do justice to it. For this is a movement which is a way of life, a civilisation and a culture, with a message that transcends the barriers of time and clime.

This book is based on lectures delivered under the auspices of the Extra-Mural Department of the University of London and Jews' College at St. John's Wood, Dollis Hill, Hammersmith and Hampstead Synagogues.

I offer it as an introduction to Hassidism and as a tribute to the memory of the hundreds of thousands of great and pious Hassidim who perished in the Nazi holocaust.

I desire to express my gratitude to my mother and to my sisters Miriam and Rachel for going over the manuscript and making many valuable suggestions that were embodied in the text. Thanks are also due to Mr. Desmond J. Trenner for his advice and constant interest in the preparation of this work and last but not least, to my wife for her great encouragement and invaluable help.

H.R.

CHAPTER I

THE BACKGROUND

The First Crusade of 1096 brought death and desolation to the flourishing and ancient Jewish communities on the Rhine and on the Moselle. The hysterical cry: 'Kill a Jew and save a soul' echoed through the blood-gashed age. The expulsion of the Jews from France in 1306, the Crusades of the Shepherds in 1320, the Black Death (1348-1351), all these factors caused the continuous influx of Jews into Poland and Lithuania.

Just as, centuries later, Turkey played the gracious host to the Spanish and Portuguese exiles, so Poland welcomed these fugitives from Germany. With its feudal system and peasantry, Poland needed people to develop her industry and commerce. As middle men, as traders, financiers, and skilled artisans, the Jews were willingly received as a vital element in the population. Expanding Poland had no room for restrictions. In 1264, Boleslav the Pious of Great Poland granted the newcomers inviolability of person and of property in a thirty-seven point charter of privileges. Discriminatory anti-Jewish enactments, which formed the fabric of Christian legislation in the neighbouring countries, were conspicuously absent in Poland. Even in disputes between Jews and Christians in the Voivode (Court), Jewish Elders acted as assistant judges.

Casimir the Great, "King of the Peasants," was also a protector of the Jews. Twice during his reign, he confirmed the Charters granted by his predecessors. His successors were less able and more erratic, but with rare exceptions the spirit of tolerance prevailed. Jews were engaged in many professions and in diverse trades. Usury, the chief Jewish occupation elsewhere in Europe, played a minor rôle in the life of Polish Jewry. They were silversmiths, tailors, printers, bakers, metal workers and innkeepers. They managed estates, collected tolls and custom dues and had the right to distil liquor. They were cattle dealers and property owners. Merchants of international standing, they imported wax from Rumania and olive oil from Italy and they played a great part in the fairs and markets of Gnesen and Lublin. The Jewish population increased from fifty thousand at the beginning of the sixteenth century to nearly half a million in the seventeenth century.

By the middle of the sixteenth century, Polish Jewry was the most highly organised Jewish community in Europe. Not since the abolition of the Patriarchate and the Exilarchs of Palestine and Babylon had Jews enjoyed so full a measure of autonomy. Every community had its own *Kahal* (Council) and elections were held during the Intermediate Days of Passover. Elders, usually called *Parnassim* or *Roshim*, were elected. They acted in rotation and had extensive powers over the community. They regulated every phase of life, from the assessment and collection of taxes to the supervision of *Talmud Torot* and cemeteries and the selection of a *Shtadlan* (Intercessor) to intervene with the king or plead with the nobles.

Local and District Councils were in turn subject to

the supreme authority known as the 'Council of the Four Lands,' *Va'ad Arba Aratzot,* embracing Little Poland (Cracow and Lublin), Great Poland (Posen), Volhynia, (Ostrog and Kremnitz), Ruthenia (Podolia and Galicia) and, for a while Lithuania (Brest and Grodno). The Council was composed of thirty delegates, six of whom were rabbis. They met periodically at the fairs of Jaroslav and Lublin. The power and the resources of the State were behind the Jewish communal organisation. The Rabbinate had full authority, almost as in the days of Hillel and Shammai.

The *Pinkas* volumes published by Simon Dubnow and Israel Halperin[1], throw much light on the diversity of Rabbinic activities in sixteenth and seventeenth century Poland. Nothing escaped their surveillance. While they dealt with political and financial matters, the rabbis exerted their influence to improve the religious and ethical standard of the community.

This elaborate organisation, this "State within a State", gave a great impetus to Torah education. "In no country," records Nathan Neta Hannover, the Polish Jewish chronicler, with justifiable pride, "was the study of the Torah so widespread among Jews as in the Kingdom of Poland. Every Jewish community maintained a Yeshiva and paid its president a high salary to enable him to conduct the institution without financial worry and to devote himself entirely to the pursuit of learning. ... Moreover, every Jewish community supported college students and allotted them a certain amount of money each week so that they might study under the direction of the president. .... The (poor) boys obtained their food either from the charity fund or from the public kitchen. A community of fifty Jewish families would support no less than thirty of these young men and boys, one family supplying board for one college student and his two pupils, the former sitting at the family table like one of the sons ... There was scarcely a house in the whole Kingdom of Poland where the Torah was not studied, and where either the head of the family or his son or his son-in-law, or the Yeshiva student boarding with him, was not an expert in Jewish learning; frequently, all of these could be found under one roof. For this reason every community contained a large number of scholars, a community of fifty families having as many as twenty learned men."[2]

The encouragement and support given by the authorities to Torah education produced rich dividends. Polish Jewry brought forth a galaxy of distinguished rabbis who made outstanding contributions to the exploration of the "sea of the Talmud" and the elucidation of the Codes.

But this golden epoch was of brief duration. Polish oppression of the Ukraine soon brought its nemesis. The absentee Polish landlord and his Lithuanian counterpart were poor statesmen. Their concern was with the present and not the future. The peasants were treated as slaves. They had many burdens and no rights. For there were differences of faith, ethnic origin and language. The masters were Catholics, the serfs were Greek Orthodox. All kinds of abuses were practised without redress. The landlords farmed out their domains to commissars who wrenched exorbitant rents from the peasantry.

The climax came under the leadership of a peasant called Bogdan Zinovi Chmielnicki (1595-1675) whose farm had been burnt down and whose infant son had been slain by an arrogant Polish overlord. Encouraged by their priests, an unholy trinity of Tartars, Cossacks

14

and peasants wreaked vengeance on the Jews, whom they regarded as the agents and allies of their oppressors. Hell was unleashed and a reign of terror began for the "heretical Pole and unbelieving Jew." In the words of a Russian historian : "killing was accompanied by barbarous tortures—the victims were flayed alive, split asunder, clubbed to death, roasted on coals or scalded with boiling water. Even infants at the breast were not spared. The most terrible cruelty, however, was perpetrated against the Jews. They were destined to utter annihilation, and the slightest pity shown to them was looked upon as treason. Scrolls of the Law were seized from the Synagogues by the Cossacks, and vilely desecrated. Then Jews were laid down upon them, and butchered without mercy. Thousands of Jewish infants were thrown into wells, or buried alive."

Barbaric and bestial were the atrocities committed by the bloodthirsty Cossacks. Maidens and mothers were violated in public. The massacre of Nemirov (Sivan 20) and in Tulchin added crimson pages to the already overfilled volumes of Jewish martyrology. More than six hundred Jewish communities were wiped out and more than a hundred thousand Jews perished in the holocaust.

For the first time in history, Polish Jewish refugees, later to become a familiar sight, began to make their way to different countries; to Holland, Italy, Turkey, and even Egypt. All the *Kahals* were in debt. Poverty was universal. The rehabilitation of stricken Jewry was retarded by the Russian and Swedish Invasions (1654-1658) and by the revival of Blood Libels. Between 1700 and 1760 no fewer than twenty of these accusations were made in Poland[3].

With the wild war cry "A Pole and a dog and a Jew on

one pole," the murderous Haidamack gangs destroyed many Jewish lives. In the words of Rabbi Moses Rivkes, author of *Beer ha-Golah* (the Well of Exile): "Throughout the whole of Lithuania, there then roamed bands of Russians and Cossacks, who devastated the cities and occupied, among others, Plock, Vitebsk and Minsk. Wherever the Cossacks appeared, in their lust for spoil, they seized all the belongings of the Jews, whom they slaughtered in masses." The glory had departed from Polish Jewry as a result of this Third Destruction.

GLIMMER OF HOPE

Intrinsic in the Jewish faith is the belief in a personal Messiah who will fulfil the Biblical prophecies and gather together the scattered remnants of the House of Israel. Rabbinic writings amplify the veiled allusions in the Bible, Apocrypha and Pseudepigrapha. Every successive persecution and calamity made the concepts of eschatology clearer. A twofold Messiah was envisaged: Messiah ben Joseph who would fight against Gog and Magog and Messiah ben David who would establish God's kingdom. A glorious era would begin and compensate in full for the hardships and bitterness of the past. Many legends were woven round the key figures of the Messianic age, the warrior-king David and the invisible but ubiquitous prophet Elijah, precursor of the Messiah. Belief in the Messiah is one of the Thirteen Articles of Faith compiled by Moses Maimonides (1135-1204) and repeated every day by devout Jews: "I believe with a perfect faith in the coming of the Messiah and though he tarry, I will wait daily for his coming."

16

Like shooting stars, false Messiahs flashed across the sky of Jewish history; but they kept the flame of Messianism glowing through the darkness of the Jewish exile.

According to the Besht, Shabbetai Zevi (1626-1676), king of the Pseudo-Messiahs, was endowed with a "holy spark." Jewry was spellbound by his magnetic personality and inflamed by his prophetic imagination. For they were drowning in the mounting waves of affliction and were ready to grasp at a straw. Shabbetai Zevi's marriage to Sarah, the Polish orphan who had lost her parents in the massacres, the prophecies of Nathan of Gaza, Elijah of the movement, the initial enthusiasm of Nehemiah Cohen—these convinced many who had hesitated before. Effective, too, was his wooing of Polish Jewry. "Soon I will avenge you," ran his message, "and comfort you even as a mother comforteth her son and recompense you a hundred-fold for the sufferings you have endured." Shabbetai Zevi claimed that the Messiah ben Joseph had preceded him in the guise of the Polish Jew Abraham Alman, who was murdered by the Cossacks.

Shabbetai Zevi preferred a Turkish turban to a martyr's death. He became a convert to Islam and was known as Mehemet Effendi, His Turkish Majesty's pensioner. He saved his own life but brought despair to the thousands who had pinned their hopes on him.

The volcano suddenly subsided but cinders were scattered far and wide. Pygmies tried to tread where the giant had failed. Hayyim Malak, Judah Hassid of Dubno, Mordecai of Eisenstadt (d. 1729), Nehemiah Hiyya Hayun (1650-1726), each in turn claimed the mantle of Shabbetai Zevi. But the most degenerate of all was Jacob Leibowicz Frank, clerk and travelling salesman turned Messiah. Sexual excesses and immoral orgies

17

took the place of mystic meditation. In a declaration to the Bishop Dembovski of Kameniec-Podolsk, he declared: "The Talmud pretends to be an interpretation of the Bible, but it is full of lies, baseness and opposition to the Torah itself. It enjoins its adherents not only to deceive Christians, but also to destroy them." Jewry sighed with relief when nearly seven hundred Frankists embraced Christianity.

SOCIAL CONDITIONS

In Eastern Europe class divisions were clear-cut. The scholars and the ignorant masses had as little in common as the nobles and the peasants. They worshipped the same God but walked different ways. There was no contact between the *Talmid Haham* who had graduated from the Yeshiva and the *Am Ha'aretz* whose college was the market place; one was preoccupied with the academic disputes of Abaye and Raba, the other with the mundane problems of existence. The students in the Beth Hamidrash, living within the "four ells of Halacha", were transported into a world of *Tannaim, Amoraim, Geonim* and the great rabbis of other times and climes. The Halacha sharpened their intellect and the Aggada gave them spiritual strength. The power of the *Kahal* was weakening. The reins were in the hands of a few wealthy oligarchs who were indifferent to the lot of the poor.

Rabbi Joseph-Yoshke, Rabbi of Dubno at the end of the seventeenth century, gives a graphic account of prevailing social conditions. "They live in luxury and splendour" (he wrote in *Yesod Yoseph*), "and do not fear the burden of taxes and other communal levies. They impose heavy burdens upon others and lighten their own burdens. They take the lion's share of all honours and distinctions ... and the congregation of God, the children of Abraham, Isaac and Jacob, are crushed and humiliated, left naked and bare-footed by the burden of heavy taxes. The tax collectors come to their homes and cruelly extort payment and rob them of all they find. They are left naked and without any utensils and clothing for wife and children. Everything is removed and sold to cover the taxes. The straw is taken out from the beds of the poor and they are left in the cold and rain, shivering and crying, each in his corner—husband, wife and children."[4]

The Yishuvniks (country people) were at the mercy of the squires. They had neither stability nor security. The saying current at the time: "One never sees a smiling peasant in Poland," applied equally to the Jews in the eastern provinces. They lived in small groups completely isolated from the main centres of Jewish life.

Social contacts were restricted. The sexes were segregated. Adults prayed separately, children played separately. Child marriages were common. It was not until 1761 that the Lithuanian Council forbade rabbis to officiate at weddings of boys under thirteen and girls under twelve. Under these circumstances, the *Shadchan*, (marriage broker), was indispensable. In vain, Jonah Landsofer, a seventeenth-century writer, pleaded: "Whenever you are arranging a marriage between two parties, never exaggerate, but always tell the literal truth." The Hebrew word for *Shadchan* was taken as an acrostic, *Sheker dover, Kesef notel*, (though speaking falsely, he taketh money).[5] The Polish Council fixed the commission at two and a half per cent of the dowry in a local marriage and at three per cent if the couple lived at a distance of more than forty-five miles.

The rabbi in Poland was a salaried official. His status was high and his economic position relatively secure. Yet there was no bond, no communication between him and the lowly members of his community. He lived in their midst, but was not one of them. They consulted him on ritual matters, but he played no part in their day-to-day life. He rarely preached to them. The sermon was reserved for *Shabbat Ha Gadol* (the Sabbath preceding Passover) and *Shabbat Shuva* (the Sabbath before the Day of Atonement). It was neither on a theme they could understand, nor in a language they could follow. It was usually a *pilpul* (dialectical discourse) on some abstruse talmudic passage or an endeavour to harmonise two conflicting statements of Maimonides. "They make it their custom to display the subtleties of their learning and their hair-splitting casuistries," says Rabbi Jacob Joseph of Polona. The scholars were spellbound, but to the masses it meant little, if anything. Later, great *Maggidim* (popular preachers) arose, like Rabbi Jacob Kranz, the Dubner Maggid, who edified, educated and even entertained their followers every Shabbat afternoon. Humility was no characteristic of the spiritual leaders, according to the testimony of the Poloner. "Everyone is hungry for power and cries out: 'I want to rule, for I am a greater scholar'."[6]

To attend a Yeshiva in the eighteenth century was the privilege of a minute minority. For the great majority, the only source of instruction was the *Cheder* or the *Talmud Torah*. The philosopher Solomon Maimon (1754-1800) gives a well-known description. "The school is commonly a small, smoky hut, and the children are scattered, some on benches, some on the bare earth. The master, in a dirty blouse, sits at the table, holding between his knees a bowl in which he grinds tobacco into snuff with a huge pestle like the club of Hercules, while at the same time he wields his authority . . . The ushers give lessons, each in his own corner, and rule those under their charge quite as despotically as the master himself . . . Here the children are imprisoned from morning to night and have not an hour to themselves except on Friday and a half-holiday at the New Moon."[7] The Baal Shem's disciple, Rabbi Jacob Joseph, similarly criticises the teacher: "He finds it more profitable to flatter and amuse the parents than to teach the children."[8] It was not surprising that the Torah, especially in the isolated parts of Poland, was a closed book to the people.

In Podolia and Volhynia, where the massacres were still fresh in the minds of men bewildered by the false trails of the pseudo-Messiahs, superstition was rife. Amulets were popular and even magic was invoked. Stories of devils and *dybbukim* were current. "There is no country where the Jews are so much given to mystical fancies, devil hunting, talismans and exorcism of evil spirits as they are in Poland,"[9] records and eighteenth century writer. Study of the Kabbala was in fashion. "Many among the masses of the people pounce upon the study of the Kabbala . . . even ordinary burghers who cannot distinguish between their right hand and their left, who walk in darkness and who cannot easily explain a simple talmudic argument or a section of the Bible even with aid of Rashi, rush to study the Kabbala."[10]

Popular too was the *Kav ha-Yosher* (the Measure of Righteousness) of Rabbi Zevi Hirsch Kaidanover (1654-

1712) with its stories of demons and *gilgulim* (the transmigrations of souls). Then men appeared who were known as *Baalei Shem* (Masters of the Name). They were itinerant preachers, who performed miracles, healed the sick and drove out *dybbukim*. Among them were Elijah of Chelm, Joel ben Isaac Heilprin, Elijah ben Moses Loans, and Sechiel Loeb Wormser, the Baal Shem of Michaelstadt.

The Jews of Podolia, Volhynia and Moldavia were surrounded by an ocean of hatred and the sky was overcast by clouds of mediaeval superstition. A guide was needed to lead the bewildered generation through the maze, to comfort and to strengthen them. In answer to this need, the Baal Shem Tov arose and walked the earth.

CHAPTER II

RABBI ISRAEL BAAL SHEM TOV

More has been written about Rabbi Israel Baal Shem Tov (the Besht) than about any other eighteenth century Jewish personality. Hardly two hundred years have elapsed since his death; yet he seems to belong to antiquity. More legends have been woven around the Besht than around Moses, father of the prophets. Facts and fiction are so interwoven that biographers find it difficult to distinguish romance from reality. Despite our lack of authentic data regarding his parentage, early upbringing and family life, the Besht is no shadowy figure. Imagination has filled the gaps and clothed him with a personality that will live forever in the hearts of his people.

Israel was born in 1700, in Okup, a small town on the borders of Volhynia and Podolia, which for a time belonged to Turkey. According to tradition, his father Eliezer lived in captivity for many years. Throughout his exile, he remained loyal to his faith and the nobility of his character was equalled by his piety. To Eliezer, saintly scholar, was promised a son destined to "enlighten the eyes of all Israel."

Eliezer and his wife died when their son was very young. But they endowed him with fine qualities: wisdom, piety, courage, optimism and a great love of nature and humanity. "And it came to pass, after the death of the Besht's father, that the lad grew up and the Jews of the community dealt kindly with him. They therefore put him in the charge of a teacher for instruction and he made rapid progress in his studies. It was a habit of his, however, to study for several days and then to run away from school. Then they would have to search for him and would find him sitting alone in the forest. They ascribed this to the fact that he was an orphan, that he had no one to look after him. They would therefore bring him back again to his teacher. And so it happened a number of times; he would run away to the woods in order to be alone, until finally they lost interest and abandoned the plan of giving him a teacher. And thus the lad grew up in an unusual manner."[11]

With great and growing intensity young Israel loved nature, loved people. He was particularly fond of children and became a *behelfer* (teacher's assistant). He did not need the *kantchik* (the whip), the then traditional weapon of the teacher, but won the hearts of his small charges by kindness. They were no longer dragged or driven to the Hebrew school. Every morning, they were led singing to *cheder*. No wonder Hassidim say that this daily procession of children singing on the way to *cheder* was as pleasing to the Almighty as the songs of the Levites in the Temple of Jerusalem.

To eke out a bare existence, the Besht worked as *shammos*, teacher, *shochet*, innkeeper and driver for his brother-in-law. But it was as a teacher that he won the affection of the people. They loved him for his patience and gentleness with the children. They asked him to settle local disputes, for he was a peacemaker by nature. And it was in the course of an arbitration that he met

Rabbi Ephraim of Kuty. The latter was so impressed by his legal acumen and sense of fair play that he offered him his daughter in marriage.

Israel spent many years in seclusion, studying, contemplating. The wide open spaces of the Carpathian mountains filled him with the knowledge of the glory of God. Though solitary, he was never alone. For he was always in the presence of God. Hassidim relate that his teacher was none other than Ahiya of Shiloh, the teacher of Elijah. He mastered the healing properties of herbs as he studied the teachings of the great masters of Kabbala: Rabbi Simeon bar Yohai, mystic and presumed author of the *Zohar*, Bible of the Kabbala, and Rabbi Isaac Luria "the Holy Lion", father of practical Kabbala. Israel interpreted these teachings with rare insight, and every utterance was stamped with his own personality.

By the year 1736, he was known in his home town as the Baal Shem Tov (abbreviated to Besht), the kind Master of God's Name. At first he followed the conventional pattern of the wandering wonder-workers, who wrote amulets (*Kemeiot*), exorcised demons, prescribed *Segullot* (magical healing aids) and healed the sick. Yet he did not affect eccentric mannerisms. He did not cloak himself in mystery in order to overawe the poor and humble. Israel was the kindest, the most approachable of men. He was a man of the people, born and bred among them, and there were no barriers between him and the masses. But preoccupation with the affairs of the moment never blurred his vision, never weakened his purpose. Healing and miracles were incidental to his mission.

After a short stay at Tluste, the Besht settled in Mied-

zyboz, near Brody, Podolia. His energy no longer dissi-
pated by tiring journeys, he was able to propound his
doctrines and to put his precepts into practice. Kabbala is a double-edged weapon. Its theories are obscure
and complex. Doctrines that deal with the mysteries of
Heaven can be misused on earth and are dangerous in
the mouths of charlatans and megalomaniacs. It was the
aim of the Besht to spread this knowledge to the
people, in such a manner that all might understand the
revelation. Every Israelite has the right to share this
knowledge of the Divine mysteries. He used Kabbalistic
terminology, but as in the vision of Ezekiel's "dry bones",
sinews, flesh, and the breath of life resurrected the
abstractions until they rose up as living realities.

Writing to his brother-in-law, Rabbi Abraham
Gershon, the Besht makes this startling revelation: "On
Rosh Hashanah, 1747, I experienced an uplifting of the
soul and I asked the Messiah, 'Let me know, Master,
when thou wilt appear on earth?' and the reply was:
'This shall be a sign unto thee, when thy teachings shall
become known ... when all other men shall have the
power of performing the same mysteries as thyself ... the
time of great favours and salvation shall arrive'." On
another occasion, the Besht himself thus summarised his
doctrines succinctly: "I have come unto this world to
show man the way in which to make the observance of
three rules his aim in life, namely, Love of God, Love of
Israel and Love of the Torah."

There are no divisions between the sacred and the
secular. A man's soul is a reflection of the *Sefirot*
(Emanations), and man must make way for the worship
of God (*Avodat Ha-Bore*) in all the acts of life. When a
man desires some material thing, such as money or

honour, he should reason thus: if my desire to attain material things, which are passing and ephemeral, is so strong, how much more ought I to desire to worship God who is Eternal, the source of lasting pleasure. "I place God before me always" (Psalms XVI. 8), was the principle he lived by. God is everywhere. He is with the scholar in the Synagogue and with the farmer in the field, for there are no veils between Man and his Creator. "No place is free of Him." The Shechina permeates all four orders: inanimate things, plants, living creatures and man. It is inherent in all creatures in the universe, whether they are good or bad.[12] God revealed himself to Moses in a bush of thorns as proof that His radiance might be glimpsed anywhere and everywhere. The world is a mirror in which the glory of God is reflected. "Naught drops into a void, neither words nor voice, but all have their fountainhead and destiny." The love of God should be entirely selfless. "If I love God, what need have I of the reward of the world to come?"

The Besht has often been described as a pantheist. However, he had little in common with Benedict de Spinoza (1632-1677). Spinoza believed in *Deus sive natura*, the identification of God and nature, so that there was no distinction between Creation and Creator. He denied the possibility of a transcending Deity, of a divine pattern and purpose. Spinoza's theories on the nature of prophecy, the miracles and the Divine origin of the Torah, have earned him the epithets "atheist", "ethical nihilist", "dialectical materialist". "Spinoza's world is a world which goes on existing beyond the life which the individual man or woman has lived and beyond the death which the individual man or woman is going to die ... The Hassidic world is the concept of a world as it is in this moment of a person's life; it is a world ready to be a sacrament, ready to carry a real act of redemption."[13]

The Besht was no casuistic philosopher. He was not concerned with matter, motion, space, energy, ultimate particles and infinite magnitudes. Nor was he concerned with speculative metaphysics. He abhorred abstractions. He spoke directly to the masses in a language they understood and he taught them piety in practical terms. His methods were even more novel than his teachings. The anecdote, the parable, the metaphor, took the place of the *pilpul*, and he appealed to the heart, not to the intellect. Not since the development of the aggada and midrashim, had the story been given such importance. To speak of the Baal Shem Tov is to speak in stories.

Though a child of the Kabbala, the Besht rejected its asceticism. Mortification, self-affliction, fasting, these were not the way to achieve the desired end. "The earlier generations," he stated, "were of a different cast, but we will not obtain communion with God in this manner." He sternly rebuked his disciple Rabbi Jacob Joseph of Polona for his behaviour: "I hear," he writes to him, "that you regard it as imperative to undergo penance and fasts. My soul is outraged ... I order you to abandon such dangerous practices ... Fast no more than that which is ordained." Fasting is the father of morbidity, of melancholy, of sadness. God can be served at the table as at the altar. Self-affliction is the ruse of the Satan to weaken a man's will. The Besht repeatedly stressed the joy to be derived from day-to-day life. God hates sadness and rejoices in the happiness of His children.

He practised what he preached. To watch the Besht praying was an unforgettable religious experience. His son (Zevi) would relate that his father appeared to him once in the shape of a fiery mountain. "Why do you appear in a shape such as this?" he asked. "In this shape I serve God," was the reply. On one occasion, he refused to enter a house of worship. "I cannot go in there; the place is full of prayers and supplications." To his puzzled disciples he explained: "The prayers recited here were uttered in a lifeless and mechanical manner. They had no wings. They never reached the higher spheres. They are choking this House of God. There is no room for me."

The accent on sincerity and spontaneity led occasionally to the disregard of the regulated times of services. *Hitlahavut* (enthusiasm) and ecstasy took the place of frigid forms of worship. The verse: "All my bones shall say, Lord, who is like unto thee!" (Psalms XXXV. 10) was taken literally. The Besht was not insensitive to criticism. He used to tell the parable of a deaf man who was once passing by a house. He looked through the window and a strange spectacle appeared to him. He saw people dancing. But he could not hear the music nor see musicians. Therefore the movement of the dancers were strange and inexplicable to him.

Rabbi Israel Baal Shem loved his fellow-men. For the people of Israel are God's treasure, His chosen people, and in every Israelite there is a spark of holiness. Absolute evil does not exist. Even an evil man is not bad through and through; there is yet a seed of goodness in him. God can be served even by an evil impulse, if the passion and the flame are turned towards God. Everything in this world is basically, intrinsically good. It is one's duty to look for the goodness and virtue in a fellow being. A man is endowed by nature with two eyes; one eye to see his neighbour's virtues, and the other to view his own fail-

ings. "What do you advise me to do with my son, he is
a real *rasha* (villain)?" asked a despairing father. "Love
him all the more," advised the Baal Shem. "God dwelleth
with them in the midst of their uncleanliness." No one
must be thrust out of the fold. He lamented the apostasy
of the Frankists. "As long as the limbs are attached to
the body, there is always the possibility of a cure. Once
amputated they can never be restored. Every member of
the House of Israel is a limb of the *Shechina*." "Fire
and brimstone," belonged to the itinerant *maggidim*
(preachers). The Besht brought no news of "Hell" and
its horrors. "God does not look on the evil side, how
dare I?"

Humility is a quality to be cultivated, and to walk in
true humility is the first duty of every Hassid. A tree,
rich in fruits, is dragged down to earth by its fruits and
its branches hang downwards. Only a branch that is
barren and withered stands upright, without bending.

It is a popular misconception that the Besht disap-
proved of study. He disliked study for ulterior motives.
"A man should study the Torah to become a Torah." The
Torah, the living words of the Most High, must influence and mould the character of the student. In the words
of the Mishna, it should "clothe him in meekness and
reverence". *Kavanah* and *Hitlahavut* were as necessary
in study as in prayer. But intellectual pride is the nega-
tion of Torah study.

The Besht, as far as we know, did not sit at the feet of
teachers of halacha. He did not spend his years in a
Yeshiva, nor did he write learned works. According to
his detractors, he was not steeped in erudition. But to
judge from his penetrating comments on the Torah, his
knowledge of the Talmud and his familiarity with Kab-

balistic works, the Master was "naturally learned." Rare intellect and innate intelligence more than compensated for lack of "book knowledge."

The Besht had tremendous power over his disciples. They loved him, they revered him, they all but worshipped him. Rabbi Leib Sarah, a contemporary of the Besht said : "If he had lived in the time of the prophets, he would have become a prophet. If he had lived in the age of the Patriarchs, he would have become an outstanding man, so that just as one says 'God of Abraham, Isaac and Jacob' one would say 'God of Israel'."

On Sivan 7th., 1760, Israel Baal Shem Tov died, surrounded by his family and his devoted disciples. His last words were in character : "Let not the foot of pride overtake me." With this verse from the Psalms, he was gathered to his fathers.

CHAPTER III

THREE GREAT TEACHERS

So Hassidism took root, but it was a tender plant. At first the movement was local, confined mainly to Podolia and Volhynia. To capture Lithuania and Poland, a new leader was needed, one who could speak the language of the scholars. Only a rabbi, trained in rabbinical schools, could influence the Jewish classicists. Among the sixty-nine disciples that tradition ascribes to the Besht, a number were outstanding talmudic scholars. The unlearned Master captured Princes of the Torah and held them spellbound.

The Besht had two children; a daughter, Adel, mother of Rabbi Baruch of Miedzyboz, and a son, Rabbi Zevi. The survival of his movement meant more to him than the survival of his dynasty. Like Moses, his successor was a stranger. His Joshua was Rabbi Dov Baer, *maggid* of Meseritz (Mezhirichi).

Dov Baer was born in 1710, in Lukatsch (Volhynia). He was the son of a poor teacher, Rabbi Abraham, and at a very early age, he exhibited a great aptitude for learning. He was sent to the Yeshiva at Lemberg where he studied under Rabbi Jacob Joshua.

Eventually Dov Baer settled in Tulchin where he became first a teacher, then a preacher; later he was a *maggid* in Korzec and Dubno. Rabbi Dov Baer was a brilliant preacher. He possessed great knowledge and powers of lucid exposition. With parables of human life, he explained abstruse passages in the Talmud and midrashim. And with his stories he shed light where there was darkness.

His work as an itinerant preacher did not prevent him from studying the Kabbala. The *Zohar* and the *Etz Hayyim* were his constant companions. He adhered rigidly to the Lurian doctrines. Fasting and mortification were his daily routine and his health suffered seriously. He went to the Besht to find a cure for his stricken body and found a new teacher who refreshed his soul. "You expound correctly," the Besht told him. "But you have no true knowledge, because there is no soul in what you know." Rabbi Baer recognised the truth of this assessment. The alumnus of the Lemberg Yeshiva, the preacher of Dubno, Rabbi Dov Baer crouched at the feet of the Besht to listen and to learn. "He taught me the language of the birds and of the trees. He revealed to me the secrets of the saints and the mystic spells,"[14] he said. And the Master perceived that his pupil was erudite and eloquent and that he possessed the qualities that his successor needed.

After the death of the Besht, the new leader settled in Meseritz. "On the day our master died," one of his colleagues said, "the Divine Presence journeyed to Meseritz."

Poor health restricted Rabbi Dov Baer to Meseritz. But what he was unable to do personally, he achieved through his disciples. He attracted a number of outstanding followers. Seldom has so much talent been gathered together in one single small town. Most of his disciples later became famous Hassidic Rabbis, founders of great

3

dynasties. His court was a school, a training ground for future *Zaddikim*. The disciples held him in great awe. Rabbi Shneur Zalman had this to say: "In the house of my teacher, the holy Maggid, you drew up holy spirit by the bucketful and miracles lay around under the benches, only no one had the time to pick them up."[15]

What the Besht achieved through stories, the Maggid achieved through discourses. He formulated a Hassidic philosophy. In the three books published by his disciple, Rabbi Solomon of Lutzk (d.1813), the Maggid expounds his conception of the Deity, his views on the Cosmology, the doctrine of the *Zaddik* and the edification of the Soul. He, too, would explain abstract ideas by means of parables.

Missionary zeal has never been a hallmark of Judaism. But as far as fellow Jews were concerned, Hassidism became a 'missionary' movement. Rabbi Dov Baer sent disciples far and wide, to spread Hassidic ideas to remote villages and towns in Poland and Lithuania. Solomon Maimon testified to the success of these 'missionaries'. "They wandered from town to town and everywhere they sought out many with heart and flesh and then turned them to God and urged them to go to Meseritz. Thus they performed great deeds and aroused the spirit of their hearers."[16]

When Rabbi Dov Baer died on Kislev 19th., 1772, twelve years after his Master, the movement had adherents in many parts of the country. Even Vilna was not without Hassidim. The Maggid left a saintly son, Rabbi Abraham 'the Angel', who succeeded him. There are conflicting reports as to the number of the Maggid's disciples. Many say he had as many as three hundred, whilst

others put the figure as low as thirty-nine. The movement branched out and the epoch of single leadership
was at an end.

RABBI JACOB JOSEPH OF POLONA

Rabbi Jacob Joseph Katz of Polona (Polonoye) played
a great part in the development of Hassidism. While the
Besht gave birth to the movement and the Maggid developed and organised it, Rabbi Jacob Joseph brought
forth a new literature.

Rabbi Jacob Joseph, like the Maggid, received a
traditional Jewish education. Scion of an illustrious
family stemming from Rabbi Samson ben Pesach Ostro-
poli (d. 1648), and Rabbi Yom-Tov Lipman Heller (1579-
1654), author of *Tosafot Yom-Tov*, his ancestors were
famed for their mastery of both Talmud and Kabbala.
Early in life he became Rabbi in Sarograd, Volhynia.
Like the Maggid, he began by resisting the growing influence of the Besht. His conventional upbringing and
education made him hostile to the concept of the
'Popular Rebbe' but finally he, too, entered the magic
circle of the Besht's devotees.

The story is told that once when the Besht made one
of his periodical visits to Sarograd, a crowd of eager
listeners soon gathered around him, enthralled by his
stories and his sayings. Rabbi Jacob Joseph was already
in the Synagogue awaiting the worshippers for morning
service. To his bewilderment, no-one arrived. At length,
he sent the beadle to investigate. The messenger hurried
to the market place and he, too, remained to listen.
Exasperated, the rabbi went himself to find his missing

flock and it was then that he first felt the magnetism of the Besht.

His 'conversion' to Hassidism was regarded with marked disfavour by his community. He was the first Hassidic leader to suffer indignities, persecution and even expulsion. He held rabbinic posts in Raskov and Nemirov and eventually found peace in Polona.

The Besht was aware of his disciple's great potentialities and was proud of his new 'convert'. "Not for the good deeds which I may have done, do I pray Thee for a portion in the world to come," he said, "but for this Yossele (Jacob Joseph) whom I have brought nigh unto Thee."[17] On another occasion, he had this to say: "All Jacob Joseph's works are pleasing to the Creator, Praised be His name, and all his doings are in the name of God."[18]

After the death of the Master, Rabbi Jacob Joseph devoted himself to writing. He published four works: *Toledot Ya'akov Yosef* (The Generations of Jacob-Joseph), *Zofnat Pa'aneach* (Revealer of Secrets), *Ben Porat Yosef* (Joseph is a fruitful vine) and *Ketonet Passim* (Coat of many Colours).

With his intellectual approach and scholarship, Rabbi Jacob Joseph enriched the movement. Miracles and myths gave way to Hassidic homilies on the Pentateuch and midrashim. Just as the Baal Shem Tov brought the Kabbala to the masses, so his disciple brought Hassidism to the scholars. Just as the *Shivche ha-Besht* gave Israel's stories, so he quoted the Master's words in the Master's name. The formulas "I heard from my teacher", and "In the name of my teacher", occur more than two hundred and eighty times.[19]

Patience and forebearance were not characteristic of

Rabbi Jacob Joseph. He believed that attack was the best form of defence. To justify the new Hassidic approach, he felt constrained to "demolish the citadel of the rabbinate". He criticised the rabbis for their sophistry, inaccessibility and materialism: "In former times, men were engaged in piety and learning for their own sake, and not for the sake of the honours and rewards they brought. The scholar would seek out the company of the uneducated and conduct himself with modesty and humility, so as to draw them nearer to their Father in Heaven; but it is not so in this generation, when there is no bond of feeling, no unity between the learned and their less cultivated brethren." Few escaped censure. He blamed the cantors for "prolonging the services", the teachers for their obsequious ways and the Elders for their "arrogance".[20]

The works of Rabbi Joseph Jacob are a valuable guide to the social conditions of the Jews in Eastern Europe in the eighteenth century. And, even more important, they bring new depth, new dimensions to Hassidic lore. From homilies on the weekly portions of the Torah, explanations of passages from rabbinic writings, and quotations from the Besht, the student can evolve the Hassidic attitude to almost every problem. Rabbi Jacob Joseph died in 1782 in Polona. His opponents burnt his books. The Hassidim regarded them as 'Holy of Holies'. In the words of Rabbi Phineas of Koretz: "Hitherto there has been no book such as this in the world because it is Divine Torah."

RABBI LEVI ISAAC OF BERDYCHEV

"A great and holy soul has descended into the world, and it shall be an eloquent advocate for Jewry." According to Hassidic legend, Rabbi Israel Baal Shem Tov greeted the birth of Rabbi Levi Isaac of Berdychev (1740-1809) with this prophetic proclamation. Rabbi Levi Isaac fulfilled his mission. A descendant of a rabbinic family renowned for scholarship, he spent his early years in study and meditation. In Meseritz, a new world opened for him, a world in which he felt at home. In this movement he found his vocation, and for it's sake he suffered persecution and humiliation. In 1785, he found peace of mind in Berdychev, "The Jerusalem of Volhynia", where he spent twenty-four happy years.

Rabbi Levi Isaac was an optimist, with a passionate belief in the inherent goodness of man. Suffering did not embitter him. He could not "behold iniquity in Jacob nor perverseness in Israel." Just as every letter in a *Sefer Torah* is sacrosanct, so every member of the House of Israel is sacred and above reproach. It is related that he once chanced upon a Jew eating in public on the Fast of Av. "Surely," the rabbi remonstrated, "you have forgotten that today is the Ninth of Av? Or perhaps you are simply not aware that it is forbidden to eat on the Fast of Av?" "I have not forgotten what day it is and I am aware of the prohibition," was the reply. "Perhaps, my son, you are not enjoying good health and were advised by your doctor to eat?" "No, I am in excellent health." Cried the Sage aloud: "See, O Lord, what a wonderful people are Thy Jews. Even when they transgress Thy commandments, they do not stoop to utter untruths."

When he saw a driver, clad in *Tallit* and *Tefillin*, oiling the wheels of his wagon, the Rabbi exclaimed: "What a holy people is Thine! Even when they oil the wheels of their wagons, they are mindful of Thee and commune with Thee." And when he heard a thief boasting to confederates of the night's haul, the rabbi commented: "It is still a long time to *Selichot*, yet the man has already begun to confess his sins."

He was constantly striving "to love a good Jew as much as God loves a wicked one." He is reputed to have told an inveterate evil-doer: "I envy you. For if you would only repent and return wholeheartedly to the Almighty, a ray of light would go forth from every one of your transgressions, and you would be altogether luminous."

His anger was roused only in the cause of Israel, whom he defended fiercely against the itinerant *maggidim* who castigated the assembled congregation with "fire, flame and brimstone." When he heard a preacher accusing the people of a multitude of sins, he protested vigorously: "Lord of the Universe! This poor *maggid* reviles and rebukes Thy people because that is how he earns his livelihood. Give him, I beg of Thee, his daily bread and save him the necessity of defaming Thy Holy People." The Berdychever was equally distressed when he heard another Rabbi publicly admonish a congregant for the hasty and indecorous manner in which he was reciting his prayers. Said the Berdychever: "It is wrong to criticise a Jew and on such grounds. God will surely understand him, just as a loving mother understands the mumblings, seemingly unintelligible, of her little child."

On the solemn Days of Judgment, *Rosh Hashana*

39

and *Yom Kippur,* the great advocate excelled himself. The House of Israel was on trial, the Heavenly Tribunal was assembled, and Rabbi Levi Isaac prepared his case and presented it with all the skill of an experienced lawyer.

Like all great advocates, he would often use a good story to support his case. And sometimes he would call witnesses. On one occasion, on the Day of Atonement, he urged a poor and humble tailor to speak up in front of the congregation. Said the man: "I, Yankel, am a poor tailor who, the truth be told, have not been too honest in my work. I have occasionally kept remnants of cloth that have been left over, and I have occasionally missed the Afternoon Service. But Thou, O Lord, hast taken away infants from their mothers and mothers from their infants. Let us on this Day of Days be quits. Mayest Thou forgive me as I forgive Thee." Remarked the Berdychever benignly: "O Yankel, Yankel, why did you let God off so lightly!"

And when the rabbi had no case to present, he would even dare to question the validity of the Heavenly Tribunal: "Do not our Sages tell us that a person who is childless is not eligible to be a member of the Sanhedrin as he may be devoid of pity? How then are the Angels entitled to constitute a Heavenly Tribunal?"

Rabbi Levi Isaac felt at home in the Divine Presence. There were no barriers between him and His Creator. On one occasion in a famous colloquy which has been set to music, he pleaded:

"Good morning to Thee, Lord of the Universe! I, Levi Isaac, son of Sarah of Berdychev, have come to Thee in a lawsuit on behalf of Thy people of Israel. What hast

Thou against Thy people Israel? No matter what happens, it is: 'Say to the Children of Israel.' No matter what happens, it is: 'Speak to the Children of Israel!' Father dear! How many other people are there in the world? Babylonians, Persians, and Edomites! ... The Germans —what do they say? 'Our King is a king!' The English— what do they say? 'Our Sovereign is a Sovereign!' And I Levi Isaac, son of Sarah, of Berdychev, say: 'Hallowed and magnified be Thy name, O God!' "

It was said of Rabbi Levi Isaac, and it is a fitting epitaph, that he loved God and he loved Judaism, but that his love for the Jews surpassed his love for both.

CHAPTER IV

THE WRATH OF ELIJAH

Elijah ben Solomon, the *Vilner Gaon*, has left a remarkable imprint on Jewish history. Though he spent almost his entire lifetime as a recluse in the 'four ells of halacha' he was venerated by his contemporaries, and became a legend in his lifetime. From the privacy of his study he wielded extraordinary power as the greatest halachic authority of Eastern European Jewry. By reason of intellect and personality, he loomed like a colossus, head and shoulders above the great men of his generation.

Elijah was born in Vilna on April 23rd., 1720. At six and a half, he is reputed to have delivered a talmudic discourse. Elijah was a prodigy in an age when *Illuim* were almost commonplace. One of his teachers was Rabbi Moses Margalit of Kaidan, author of *P'ne Moshe*, an illuminating commentary on the *Yerushalmi* (Palestinian Talmud). At a very early age, Elijah married Hannah, daughter of Rabbi Judah of Kaidan, and she bore him two sons, Aryeh Leib and Abraham.

Elijah's capacity for study was almost superhuman. He was the *matmid par excellence*. His path was the path of the Torah and he never diverged from it. To the Torah he dedicated his life, his strength, his energy; for Torah study was the reason for his existence. Yet his knowledge was encyclopaedic and his span of interest great. He studied Hebrew grammar, mathematics, biology and medicine. He encouraged Baruch of Shklow (1752-1810) to translate into Hebrew the six books of Euclid's geometry.

Peshat (literal interpretation) rather than *Pilpul* (casuistry) was his aim. "With a single shaft of the light of truth he would illumine the darkness, and with a single word he would overthrow heaps of *pilpulim* hanging by a hair.[21]

Almost a century before *Jüdische Wissenschaft*, the Gaon of Vilna analysed rabbinic texts with scientific skill. His mastery of rabbinic literature enabled him to make many happy emendations, resolving problems that had long baffled scholars. Like his illustrious ancestor, Rabbi Moses Kraemer, the Gaon refused to make the Torah "a spade to dig with". He declined a position as rabbi and lived on a small legacy bequeathed him by Rabbi Moses Rivkes. Unlike Maimonides, whose days were occupied with the court of the Vizir Al-Kadi al-Fadil, private patients and communal affairs, the Gaon cut himself off from contemporary life.

It is one of the ironic twists of history, that the Gaon, who was himself styled 'The Hassid', became the greatest antagonist of the Hassidim. Small Hassidic groups were established in Brest-Litovsk, Grodno, Troki and Lutzk. The fiery activities of Rabbi Aaron of Karlin (near Pinsk) sent sparks flying far and wide and a spark or two landed in Vilna. There, too, the *klaus* of Karliner Hassidim headed by Rabbi Isar and Rabbi Hayyim, was beginning to attract attention. The infiltration of the Hassidim into Vilna, 'The Holy of Holies' of the Mitnagdim, was sacrilege to the Gaon and he devoted more than two decades of his life to a bitter battle against the upstart movement.

The Hassidim adopted the *Nusach Ari*, the Prayer Book of Rabbi Isaac ben Solomon Luria (1534-1572). By discarding the *Minhag Ashkenaz* (German ritual), they were of necessity compelled to establish their own Houses of Worship. And to the Gaon it seemed that the separatist tendencies of the Hassidim might disrupt and demoralise the House of Israel.

The Gaon insisted upon punctilious observance of the minutiae of all rabbinical laws and regulations. He found it unpardonable that some of the Hassidim should disregard the prescribed hours of worship. He did not believe that *devekut* and *kavanot* could make up for belated services. He was not moved by the Hassidic reasoning: "Can a child be told when he may approach his father?" Nor did he accept their thesis that spontaneity ranks higher than punctilious recitation.

The Gaon was deeply concerned with synagogal services. He himself deleted many *Piyyutim* (liturgical compositions) and encouraged communal singing. But he abhorred the undisciplined way in which many of the Hassidim were accustomed to pray, swaying and dancing, sighing and laughing, as the mood seized them. Matters were aggravated by the indecorous behaviour of the Hassidim in and around Vilna. "They poured scorn on the students of the Torah and the learned, inflicting all manner of ridicule and shame on them, turning somersaults in the street and market places of Kalisk and Liozna, and generally permitting themselves all sorts of pranks and practical jokes in public."[22]

The Gaon has been described as the 'Ewige Student'. To a man so dedicated to scholarship, no amount of

Torah-study could be adequate, let alone excessive, and in his eyes, the criticism of intensive study expressed by some of the Hassidic leaders threatened the very survival of Judaism. Neither the erudition of the Maggid nor the intellectual brilliance of the works of Rabbi Jacob Joseph of Polona could allay Elijah's fear that "the Torah would be forgotten in Israel." Passionately, he attacked the advice of the Hassidic rabbis that "a man must not accustom himself to passing all his time in study," and he was in complete disagreement with the dictum of the Besht that "the Evil Inclination, *Yetzer Hora*, persuades a man to study the Talmud with all its commentaries in order to prevent him from following other studies which might lead him to the fear of God."[23]

Hassidic leaders launched a retaliatory attack on their Rabbinic opponents, whom they accused of "exhibitionism, hypocrisy, sophistry and learning not for the sake of Heaven." Rabbi Jacob Joseph was not the only critic. Rabbi Judah Leib, the Preacher of Polona (d.1770), the author of *Kol Aryeh* (The Voice of a Lion), also censured the scholars for their pride and intellectual arrogance. "They are wise, understanding and God-fearing in their own estimation."

The cult of *Zaddikim*, too, was foreign to the Gaon, for it gave rise to a new type of teacher whose powers stemmed from the heart rather than the head. The training ground for the *Zaddik* was the court of his rabbi rather than Yeshiva, for knowledge was not the chief qualification for leadership. Discourses about *Zaddikim* took the place of Talmud discussions. Instead of poring over the tractates of the Talmud, instead of exploring the highways and byways of halacha, Hassidim discussed with awe the miracles

45

wrought by the 'Wonder Rabbis' and a rich new folk-lore grew up around these fabled figures. Many of the *Zaddikim* lived on a high spiritual level to which they could raise their followers. Among them were such rare personalities as Rabbi Menachem Mendel of Vitebsk, Rabbi Sussay of Annopal, Rabbi Phineas Shapira of Koretz (Korzec) (1726-1791) and Rabbi Meir Margulies (d.1790). But for the Vilna Gaon, out of touch with the times and blinded by prejudice, it was as if they did not exist.

Mystic though he was, the Gaon failed to recognise in the potentials and resources of Hassidism one of the last phases in the "Trends of Jewish Mysticism". In his eyes, Hassidism had more in common with Sabbatianism, Frankism and mystical heresies than with Luria's Kabbala. Elijah's knowledge of the doctrines and dogmas of Hassidism came to him from devious sources, frequently unreliable, and invariably biased. The Gaon was a child of his age. The acquisition of knowledge had been for him an intellectual exercise and had not broadened his outlook. He was intolerant of anyone whose views differed from his own.

In 1771, an epidemic broke out in Vilna and many children sickened and died. A scapegoat had to be found and the Hassidim were chosen for this rôle by the Vilna *Kahal*. They were compelled to do public penance and their *klaus* was closed. But the Gaon was not content with these penalties, severe though they were. In 1772, the Vilna *Kahal*, with the consent of the Gaon, issued a *cherem* (a decree of Excommunication) against the 'godless sect'.

The *cherem* was the most powerful weapon which the Jewish community possessed and it was generally

used in order to maintain communal discipline. In a by-
gone age, when the synagogue was the pivot of the community, the mere threat of *cherem* would often subdue
unruly elements. The awesome ceremony, complete with
wax candles, Shofar and Scrolls, was designed to strike
terror in the heart and the invocation of the *cherem*
resounded with the chill horror of a sentence of death.

But even these measures were not harsh enough for
the Gaon. "Had I the power," he said, "I would have
punished these infidels as the worshippers of Baal were
punished of old."[24]

Rabbi Shneur Zalman of Ladi and Rabbi Menachem
Mendel of Vitebsk came to Vilna and sought a personal
interview with the Gaon. But the Gaon would not consent to see them. To him they were in the category of
unbelievers, with whom all contact is strictly forbidden. In the words of Rabbi Shneur Zalman: "He shut
the doors on us twice. The leaders of the city entreated
him as follows: 'Our teacher! Their famous rabbis have
come hither to talk matters over and if the discussions
are successful peace will prevail in Israel.' But the Gaon
would not yield and when he was pressed further, he left
the town and did not return until our departure."[25]

On the Ellul 3rd., 1781, the Rabbinical Assembly
at Zelva (a province of Grodno) noted the Gaon's words:
"Although it is not my custom to trespass beyond my
province, yet I also give my signature, mindful of the
saying : 'When the Torah is being made void, it is time
to act for the Lord.' We order that a day of fasting and
public prayer be instituted on the 25th. of the month of
Tevet of the current year, the meat of their *Shechita*
is to be considered carrion, and the instruments used
are to be considered polluted and forbidden ... No com-

munity may permit any one of them to hold a position as *chazan* or rabbi and no one of them may teach our children."[26]

Both the *Toledot Ya'akov Yosef*, and the *Testament of Rabbi Israel Baal Shem* were publicly burnt. Hassidim were persecuted. Communities were divided by hatred and bitterness. Acts of violence were not uncommon. The house of the saintly Rabbi Levi Isaac was ransacked. The Kabbalist Rabbi Nachum of Czarnobyl (d.1797), disciple of the Maggid and author of *Me'or Enayim*, was actually attacked whilst preaching in the Synagogue.

In May 1794, it was related in Vilna that a Hassidic delegate was travelling the country purporting to be the son of the Gaon. In every community he loudly maintained that his father deeply regretted the harsh measures that he had taken against the Hassidim and now made atonement for his grievous errors. Fierce and fearsome was the wrath of the Gaon. In a letter addressed to the communities of Lithuania, White Russia, Volhynia and Podolia, he writes: "Ye mountains of Israel ... You hold in your hands a hammer wherewith you may shatter the plotters of evil, the enemies of light, the foes of the (Jewish) people. Woe unto this generation! They (the Hassidim) violate the law, distort our teachings, and set up a new covenant; they lay snares in the house of the Lord, and give a perverted exposition of the tenets of our faith. It behoves us to avenge the Law of the Lord, it behoves us to punish these madmen before the whole world, for their own improvement. Let none have pity on them and grant them shelter! ... Gird yourselves with zeal in the name of the Lord."[27]

Elijah of Vilna saw himself in the rôle of his namesake,

the zealous prophet of the Lord. The Hassidim were to the Gaon what the worshippers of Baal were to the prophet. In another letter dated Tishri 11th., 5557, (October 14th., 1796) he writes: "Satan has forced his way among the scattered flock of Israel and caused confusion among them ... These dolts, who have sown so much evil, should be chastised before the assembled people with whips and scorpions and brought to reason. No man shall have pity upon them and take their part, but rather shall they be cast out from all the tribes of Israel as evil-doers."

In October 17th., 1797 (Tishri 19th.), the Gaon died. Vilna was plunged into deep mourning but some of the Vilna Hassidim rejoiced over the death of their great persecutor. The community was incensed. A special committee, consisting of five members of the *Kahal*, was appointed to deal with the heretics. But two decades of relentless warfare, waged by the greatest exponent of talmudic Judaism in modern times, had failed to destroy or even weaken the movement. Stronger measures were called for. The Second and Third Partitions of Poland had taken place. Lithuania, Volhynia and Podolia were now under the jurisdiction of Russia. With the connivance of the committee, a certain Hirsch ben David, drew the attention of the Prosecutor General in St. Petersburg to the "political misdeeds perpetrated by the chief of the Karliner (Hassidic) sect, Zalman Borukhovitch (son of Baruch)".[28]

The Russians acted on this information with practised speed. In 1798, Rabbi Shneur Zalman of Ladi and twenty other Hassidim were arrested. The Hassidim were soon freed, but Rabbi Shneur Zalman was taken to St. Petersburg. On Kislev 19th., he, too, was released. His freedom

4

was short-lived. Avigdor Haimovitch, vindictive and un-scrupulous, was at one time rabbi in Pinsk. He had, how-ever, alienated the Hassidim and they had deposed him. The ex-rabbi turned informer. In a long memorandum to the Russian Emperor Paul I, he described the Hassidic sect as "a pernicious and dangerous organisation", and he supported the accusation with a wealth of dis-torted detail and malicious misquotations. Rabbi Shneur Zalman was re-arrested and taken for a second time to St. Petersburg. It was not till the Av 11th., 1801, that he left the capital of Russia a free man.

The Hassidim of Vilna were not of the stuff of which martyrs are made; the oppressive yoke of the *Kahal* lay heavily upon them and they adopted the tactics of their adversaries. On February 4th., 1799, the Elders of the *Kahal* were arrested. Eight Hassidim were elected to the Council and for a time a Hassid, Meir Raphael, was even the head of the community. The civil war was finally settled by State intervention. The Jew's Statute of 1804 granted every Jewish community the right to build sep-arate synagogues and to choose its own rabbis. The struggle was over. Hassidim and Mitnagdim had to learn to live and let live, to worship and to let others worship as each saw fit.

CHAPTER V

THE LEGACY OF HABAD

Shneur Zalman ben Baruch, the founder of Habad Hassidism, was born on Ellul 18th., 1745 in Liozna, Russia.
Little is known about his parentage and early upbringing, in sharp contrast with the wealth of detail which
surrounds every aspect of the latter part of his life.
One of his teachers was Rabbi Baer of Lubavitch. His
teacher soon felt that his brilliant pupil no longer needed
his tuition. "This young lad," he said, "is fit to be
my friend and companion, not my disciple. He needs
no guidance in the study of the Talmud. His mental
faculties are such that he can make his own way through
the 'sea of the Talmud' and its commentaries."

Even before he was *barmitzva*, Shneur Zalman became an associate of the *Chevra Kadisha* (The Holy
Society for supervising burial arrangements) and was already styled with the honorary title of 'Rabbi'. He had
a methodical mind and methodical was his acquisition of
the Torah. "When I was thirteen years old," he writes, "I
studied most of the time by myself. Eighteen hours a
day I devoted to my studies. For three consecutive years,
I allotted two-thirds of my time, during the weekdays, to
the study of the Talmud and the Codes, and the remaining third I utilised for the study of Scripture, Aggada,
Midrash and Kabbala. On the Sabbath, a third of the

day, I studied the Talmud and the Codes, a third I studied Scripture and Aggada, and a third I devoted to Midrash, Zohar and Kabbala."[29]

His reputation spread and men of wealth competed for the privilege of offering him their daughters in marriage. At the age of fifteen, the youthful scholar married Sterna, daughter of Yehuda Leib Segal of Vitebsk. But the change of personal status did not change his way of life. Nothing could quench or abate his thirst for Torah study. However, this devotion to study seemed excessive to his materialistic father-in-law, who gave vent to his resentment in mean and petty ways. He even begrudged Shneur Zalman the candles he needed in order to study at night. But the ardour of the student was not lessened. By moonlight, he continued his intensive studies of Rabbinical and mystical Judaism. At midnight and in the stillness and solitude of the dawn, the city of Vitebsk could hear the musical voice of the wakeful *matmid* as he chanted to himself.

Like the Gaon of Vilna, he devoted time to the study of astronomy, trigonometry and Hebrew grammar which he regarded as essential to the understanding of the Torah. Alone, without a colleague, without a teacher, the nineteen-year-old student became restless. He was aware that "two luminaries were shining in the world": the light of Meseritz (stronghold of the Maggid) and the light of Vilna (Mitnagdic centre). "In Vilna, Torah is studied, but in Meseritz they learn how to pray. My soul," he declared, "desired Torah. I set out for Vilna. On the way I changed my mind. For I no longer required a teacher for study but I needed a guide who would show me how to serve God. Such a counsellor would I find in Meseritz."[30]

The journey was long and arduous, but eventually Rabbi Shneur Zalman arrived in Meseritz, and here he found what he sought, a wise teacher who instructed him and inspired him. "Blessed be the Lord," he exclaimed, "who hath led me in the true path." The Maggid, like the Besht, possessed great powers of discernment and soon perceived the rare quality of his new disciple. Hassidim relate, that as the Maggid was passing through the students' dormitory one night, he paused at the bed of Rabbi Shneur Zalman, who was fast asleep. "Miracle of miracles," he said gently, "that so great a spirit lives in so frail a dwelling! How wonderful to think that this young man, now sleeping unaware on his pillow, shall one day become the rabbi of all the provinces of Russia, with multitudes of people listening to his voice."

If the master honoured the student, the disciple revered the master, and repeatedly acknowledged his indebtedness to him. "When we learned Torah from the Maggid it was as though he taught us the Oral Law. When we heard him tell a story it was as though he taught us the Written Law." The personality of the Maggid impressed itself upon him and they were constant companions. "I behold my teacher, the Maggid, when I dream and when I am awake. The Besht, however, I see only in a dream, and only on Sabbaths and festivals."

For three years, Rabbi Shneur Zalman sat at the feet of the Maggid. When the Maggid lived in Dubno and Annopal Rabbi Shneur Zalman followed. At the home of the teacher he also found colleagues of the calibre of Rabbi Elimelech of Lishensk (1717-1786), Rabbi Levi Isaac of Berdychev and Rabbi Nachum of Czarnobyl. He was generous in acknowledging his debt to these celebrated scholars. "Torah I learned from the Maggid, who was my guide in Ethics. From Rabbi Phineas Shapiro of Korzec, I learned the qualities of truth and humility. And from Rabbi Yechiel Michal of Zlotchow (1726-1780), I absorbed melodies which he had heard from the Besht himself."

Rabbi Abraham, the Maggid's son (1741-1777), was the only Hassidic leader to be called 'The Angel'. "Not in vain," remarked Rabbi Levi Isaac of Berdychev, "did they call him 'Angel', for he is as pure as his deeds." Though heir to the traditions of Hassidism, the 'Angel' spent his days in fasting, self-affliction and solitude. The Maggid entrusted his saintly son to Rabbi Shneur Zalman. For six hours a day they studied together—and both of them benefited from these studies. They devoted three hours to Talmud and three hours to Kabbala. "Let my son go his own way," was the Maggid's instruction to the tutor. "Explain the Torah to him as you understand it and he will interpret it according to his own conception. Show him the Talmud according to the letter and he will explain its meaning to you according to the spirit."[31]

Though one of the youngest and newest of the disciples, Rabbi Shneur Zalman was encouraged by the Maggid to undertake the compilation of a new *Shulchan Aruch*. Rabbi Shneur Zalman was certainly well qualified for this task. His knowledge of Rabbinic literature was allied with a gift for lucid exposition. His well-stocked and methodical mind could not tolerate ambiguity or obscurity. Maimonides was forty-five when he completed his *Mishne Torah* in 1180; Joseph Karo was sixty-seven when he finished writing the *Schulchan Aruch* in 1555; but Rabbi Shneur Zalman was only twenty-three when he completed the section *Orach Hayyim*.

The youthful codifier marshalled ancient authorities with masterly skill and thoroughness. His work won him high praise from his contemporaries. They called him 'Prince of the Torah', and declared that he was 'unique in his generation', and they said of him: "He is like an iron pillar on whom one can depend." Rabbi Shneur Zalman usually prefers the views of the Ashkenazi scholars to those of the Sephardim, just as he adopts the attitude of the halachic authorities in preference to that of the mystics. *Orach Hayyim* was an irrefutable reply to those Mitnagdim who accused the Hassidim of lightening the "yoke of the *mitzvot*". Shneur Zalman was motivated throughout by the idea that a man is duty bound to be as heedful of a minor precept as of a major precept and may not contravene even the slightest injunction of the Scribes.

When the Maggid died in 1772, there was no-one to hold the Hassidim together. The great disciples soon scattered far and wide, and many established their own 'Courts'. Rabbi Shneur Zalman, however, stayed on at Annopal and gave loyal support to his former disciple, Rabbi Abraham the 'Angel', and Rabbi Menachem Mendel of Vitebsk, the venerable disciple of the Maggid who had beheld the glory of the Besht. But it was not long before Rabbi Menachem Mendel made his way to the Holy Land and Rabbi Abraham died at the age of thirty-six. In this way Rabbi Shneur Zalman was deprived of both teacher and colleague, and he reverted to the solitary life he had led before entering the home of the Maggid. Caring little for honour or leadership, he withdrew from the world of people into the world of books. Hassidim relate that even at the age of forty, he still shrank from the homage of the people who flocked to him. His wife, however, appeased him: "They are coming,' she said, "to hear the Torah of the Maggid."

Then the Gaon of Vilna launched his mighty offensive against Hassidism and the movement, maligned and menaced, desperately needed a powerful leader. Rabbi Menachem Mendel realised this and from the Holy Land he exerted his influence. To his followers he declared that "Him (Shneur Zalman) we have anointed to be a teacher of righteousness in this country, that the Congregation of the Lord be not like sheep without a shepherd. For who is like unto him, a guide and a teacher ... You are all obliged to honour him ... He is faithful, worthy, upright and righteous."[32]

Rabbi Shneur Zalman rose to the occasion. In time of crisis, there is no room for hesitation or excessive humility. He was soon recognised as the Hassidic leader of White Russia and Lithuania, and his followers were numbered in thousands. But his new status made no difference to his way of life. He continued to live modestly and without ostentation, for he abhorred luxuries. He attributed the troubles of Israel in the Diaspora to the desire of the people for wealth and rich living.

Rabbi Menachem Mendel in *Eretz Yisrael* could do little except sympathise from afar. "We have heard," he writes, "the groaning of the children of Israel. By His Name I swear that there is not in our doctrine or beliefs any trace of blemish or uncleanliness. We forgive all those who provoke us and harm us physically and materially."[33] Rabbi Shneur Zalman, too, preached forgiveness and advocated patience. "Hide for a while until the storm passes." The die was cast, and peaceful overtures were neither appreciated nor reciprocated. Rabbi Shneur Zalman became the 'Suffering Servant' of Hassidism. Twice he was arrested and taken to St. Petersburg and his stay in the Russian capital gave rise to many legends. His noble bearing and obvious integrity were great assets and helped to establish his innocence. The dignitaries in St. Petersburg were impressed by his wisdom and ready wit.

Persecutions and sufferings did not embitter the *Zaddik*. He remained calm and kindly, and worked to the end for peace and reconciliation with his opponents. Writing to the leaders of Mogilev, he laments: "We have been sold alive. We cannot even be ransomed for money. We implore you, do not cast us aside ..." Vindictiveness was alien to him. He preferred to forgive rather than to avenge. And he tried to instil this spirit of magnanimity into his Hassidim, for their conduct was a matter of great concern to him. He endeavoured to infuse them with a sense of responsibility. The movement must not suffer for the misdeeds of individual members. A minority is always liable to be misunderstood, so the few should refrain from antagonizing the many and a high standard of Hassidic conduct was the best defensive measure Rabbi Shneur Zalman could devise. He wanted to convince, not to coerce, the Mitnagdim and to impress upon them the baselessness of their accusations. With this object in view, he visited Rabbi Moses Heifetz, Rabbi Joshua Zeitlin and Rabbi Joel of Zaslav. His learning, strong convictions and fiery eloquence could not but disprove many of the accusations levelled against the Hassidim. By tireless endeavours, Rabbi Zalman succeeded in narrowing the schism that divided the House of Israel.

Shneur Zalman was not destined to enjoy the quietude and tranquillity he loved so dearly. The phenomenal rise and the martial exploits of Napoleon brought about radical changes in the position of the Jews in Europe. As the Napoleonic armies marched through Italy, "the walls of the ghetto began to dance." The yellow badge gave place to the tricolour cockades and the ghetto gates were torn off their hinges. In 1799, while Napoleon was in the East, he is said to have invited the Jews of Asia and Africa to rally to his standards "pour rétablir l'Ancienne Jerusalem" (to re-establish the ancient city of Jerusalem). Eight years later (on February 8th., 1807), he summoned a Sanhedrin in order that it might "reveal again to the people the true spirit of its laws and render proper interpretation of all mistaken conceptions." The idea had great possibilities but, unhappily, the Paris Sanhedrin proved a dismal failure. Still, the reputation and popularity of Napoleon were high among the Jews in Poland. And he is reported as saying: "To me at least, the Sanhedrin is useful." Many Polish Jews looked upon him as the liberator of Poland.

Some of the Hassidic rabbis in Poland prayed for Napoleon. Among his staunch supporters was Rabbi Menachem Mendel of Rymanov (d. 1815). Rabbi Jacob Isaac of Lublin (d. 1815), Rabbi Israel of Kozienice (d. 1814) and Rabbi Naftali of Ropczyce (1760-1827) strongly opposed French dominion. For him, Napoleon was the symbol of heresy and agnosticism. And this was the attitude of Rabbi Shneur Zalman. He remembered with gratitude his fair treatment in St. Petersburg. In a letter, he writes: "Should Bonaparte win, the wealth of the Jews will be increased, and their (civil) status will be raised. At the same time, their hearts will be estranged from our Heavenly Father. Should, however, our Czar Alexander win, Jewish hearts will draw nearer to our

Heavenly Father, though the poverty of Israel may become greater and his status lower."[34]

To escape capture by the advancing French armies,
Rabbi Shneur Zalman left his home. "I prefer to die,
rather than live under him (Napoleon)," he writes. With
his family, twenty-eight souls in all, he departed in haste,
leaving most of his possessions behind. From Ladi, the
family journeyed to Krasny, and then to Smolensk. After
many hardships, he died in Haditz near Kursk on Tevet
24th. (December 28th.), 1813. His last words to his
family were: "Soon I will no longer be with you. My
children, do not act proudly. Do not rely upon me to
plead for you before the Heavenly Court. Do not depart,
God forbid, from the way of the Torah and the commandments."

Rabbi Shneur Zalman left a vast literary treasure
house. In addition to his *Shulchan Aruch*, he wrote *Torah
Or* (Torah Light), homilies on Genesis and Exodus;
Likutei Torah, homilies on Leviticus, Numbers, Deuter-
onomy, Esther, Lamentations and Canticles; *Bëurei ha-
Zohar* (commentary on the Zohar); *Seder Tefilla*, a prayer
book with a Kabbalistic commentary, in two volumes;
Likutei Amarim, or *Tanya*, in two parts, the first con-
taining an exposition of Hassidism, the second entitled
Sha'ar Hayichud Veha'Emuna, a commentary on the
Shema.

Rabbi Shneur Zalman has been described as the
Maimonides of Hassidism. He represents the synthesis of
Lithuanian talmudism with the passionate warmth of
the Besht. Emotion and *hitlahavut*, rich legacies of Rabbi
Israel Baal Shem Tov, are supplemented by and co-ordi-
nated with an intellectual approach. According to Rabbi
Shneur Zalman, the intellect comprises three faculties,

chochma (wisdom), *bina* (understanding) and *da'at* (knowledge). To the talmudic conception "God wants the heart", a new theory was added on the function of the mind. Heart and mind are the two portals of the heavenly spheres. Thought is elevated above feeling. The dwelling-place of the soul is in the mind. "Just as it is impossible to beget children without a mother, so it is impossible to be God-fearing without thought."

A man is neither a static nor a passive entity. He is a dynamic being endeavouring to climb higher and higher up the ladder of spirituality. There is no aristocracy in the spiritual realm and promotion is within everyone's grasp. Every Jew has the makings of a saint, for his soul has its place in the 'Divine Abode'. In the teachings of Habad, the *Zaddik* is neither an 'intermediary', nor 'a pillar of the world'. The *Zaddik* is a supervisor and not a superior, a teacher of morals and not a worker of miracles. It is well to have a support when walking, but it is preferable to walk unaided. A Habad Hassid is unique among Hassidim. He visits the Rabbi, and is guided and instructed by him, but does not efface himself before his teacher, for the bond between them is one of mutual esteem and affection. The Habad Hassid is trained to spiritual self-sufficiency and not to total dependence on the *Zaddik*.

Equally conventional was the Habad conception of study. For Habad regarded the study of the Torah as equal to the observance of all the commandments. Through the study of the Torah, man can reach the highest stage of development and self-perfection. The Torah illumines the mind and elevates the thoughts. Questioned by Rabbi Joshua Zeitlin as to the attitude of the Hassidim to Torah study, Rabbi Shneur Zalman replied: "The Hassidim, too, set aside times for study. The difference between them and the Mitnagdim is this: the latter set times for study and they are limited by a time factor, whereas the former make the Torah their path in life." The study of the Torah is food for the soul. Just as the body needs food, so the soul needs Torah. From every chapter that one studies and every *mitzva* one performs, an angel is created. He who studies the Torah or fulfils the *mitzvot* enthusiastically creates lively angels. If, however, there is no enthusiasm, the angels are lifeless and frigid. Nothing in Torah study is irrelevant or outdated.

Rabbi Shneur Zalman set his disciples high standards. A Hassid must live in the spirit of Hassidism twenty-four hours a day. He is recognised by the way he talks, by the way in which he loves Israel with his heart and with his soul. Sincerity and unselfishness are the keynotes of the Hassid. In the enlightened Hassidic philosophy, the humble are honoured and not humiliated. Shneur Zalman explains that "the burning bush (Ex. 3,2.), symbolizes the humble Jew who is burning with a passionate fire, a fire which, like that of the bush, is unextinguishable. For the scholar's passionate worship of God finds an outlet in his prayer and in his study of the Torah which enables him to blend the flame of his feelings with the coolness of his intellectual understanding; but the non-scholar finds no such relief from the continuous fire of his yearning for God. So it is from the humble bush that the voice of God speaks out."

Prayer occupies a vital position in the pattern of Habad and detailed regulations are laid down. The Service should neither be prolonged nor hurried. It should be permeated by a spirit of reverence. *Kavana* is essential to prayer. A prayer or a blessing without *kavana* is like a body without a soul.

Rabbi Shneur Zalman's faith gave his utterances a certainty and a clear-cut definition that contrasts vividly with the doubts and perplexities with which the philosophers of the eighteenth century were beset. The style of the *Tanya* is as crisp and clear as that of the Code. Rabbi Shneur Zalman avoids technical terms as much as possible and uses language which the layman can understand. And there is freshness and originality in his presentation and interpretation. The *Tanya*, the 'Bible' of Habad, was regarded by his contemporaries with great veneration. "With the *Tanya*," said Rabbi Sussya of Annopal, "the Israelites will go forth to meet the Messiah."

No other Hassidic rabbi has left so stylised an imprint on the movement as this 'Suffering Servant'. He established a dynasty (Lubavitch). He formulated a philosophy, Habad. He added fuel to the fire kindled by the Besht and the flames burned with a new and holy brilliance.

CHAPTER VI

RABBI NACHMAN OF BRATSLAV

"The Holy One blessed be He sends the cure before the malady." So says the Midrash, and this saying comes to mind when one considers the life and works of Rabbi Nachman. For Nachman was born in the very same year that the Maggid of Meseritz died and the Vilna Gaon issued his *cherem* against the Hassidim. Rabbi Nachman's personality made a great impact on his generation. He was the most gifted story-teller in the annals of Hassidism.

Nachman was born on Rosh Chodesh Nisan 1772, in Miedzyboz. His mother, Feige, was a daughter of Adel, the Besht's only daughter. His father, Rabbi Simcha, was the son of Rabbi Nachman of Horodenka, a follower of the Besht. But genius is not hereditary and the descendants of the Besht did not inherit the remarkable qualities of their great ancestor. Of the grandchildren of the Besht, Rabbi Moses Chayyim Ephraim of Sudylkov (1745-1800), the author of *Degel Machnei Ephraim* (the Banners of the Camp of Ephraim), was a fine scholar of retiring disposition, while Rabbi Baruch of Miedzyboz (1757-1811) was quarrelsome, boastful and exceedingly vain.

Unaffected by the fratricidal struggle that raged between the Hassidim and the Mitnagdim in Lithuania, Nachman spent his childhood in assiduous study. The glory of the Besht had not departed from Miedzyboz. Everything there reminded him of his great grandfather and he spent many hours at the ancestral tomb, seeking guidance and inspiration. Little Nachman learned fast. At the age of six, he was reputed to be in earnest struggle to overcome his sensual desires. He studied Talmud, Bible, *Zohar* and the writings of the Kabbalists with increasing avidity. When Nachman was thirteen, his uncle, Rabbi Moses Chayyim Ephraim, predicted that he would be "the greatest of all the *Zaddikim*." That year, he married the daughter of Ephraim Baer of Medvedevka and for a time lived in Husiatyn, Podolia.

Nachman did not believe in short cuts to Heaven. Great grandson of the Besht though he was, he adopted the methods of Luria. Though suffering from a tubercular malady, he indulged in prolonged fasts that often lasted a whole week. In one twelve-month period, he fasted 'from Sabbath to Sabbath' on eighteen occasions. His deep concern for the well-being of his Hassidim contrasted sharply with his indifference to his own health. Periods of self-mortification would be followed by immersion, in icy cold *mikvaot* (pools for ritual immersion).

Premonitions of his short span of life were always with him. Not an hour was wasted and not a minute lost. He regarded every single day as if it were his very last. Nor did he rest on the spiritual laurels of his distinguished ancestor. "The world imagines," he said, "that because I am a descendant of the Besht, I have attained a high status. It is not so. I have succeeded because I have afflicted my body. Whatever I have achieved, is due to my own endeavours."

He was a complex and colourful personality, endowed with a high degree of sensitivity. Once he spent the night

in a newly-built wooden cabin, and slumber fled from
his eyes. "I could not close my eyes all night," he related
next morning. "I felt the groaning of the timbers. They
wailed and moaned because they had been cut off before their time." The temperamental Rabbi alternated
between periods of deep depression and high exultation.

Rabbi Nachman was a great lover of *Eretz Yisrael*. He
is Hassidism's greatest Zionist. "All Holiness comes by
way of the Holy Land. Only there is it possible to ascend
the ladder of holiness. The holiness of *Eretz Yisrael* aids
in the attainment of faith and patience; and it strength-
ens the resolutions to do away with anger, melancholy
and heaviness of heart."[35] Aphorisms were no substitute
for action. In 1798, at the age of twenty six, he decided
to undertake the journey. In vain his daughter pleaded
with him: "Who will look after us while you are in *Eretz
Yisrael?*" He was unswerving in his determination. "Go
to your parents-in-law; your elder sister will become a
servant. People will have pity on your younger sister.
Your mother will become a cook. I will sell the household goods to provide the means for the journey."

Despite the pitiful plight of his family, his frail constitution and the troubled state of the Middle East, Rabbi
Nachman set out on his journey in Iyar 1798. The
journey was indeed long and wearisome but he eventually arrived in Haifa on the eve of Rosh Hashana 1799.

In *Eretz Yisrael* the sensitive Rabbi was in his element.
He claimed that he had attained a high degree of spirituality after walking four cubits on the soil of the Holy
Land. What Yehuda Halevi (1085-1142) achieved in
poetry, Rabbi Nachman expressed in prose. He produced
a great many memorable aphorisms. He stayed in Haifa
and Tiberias. He visited the graves of his spiritual

63

teachers, the Kabbalists. Wherever he went Rabbi Nachman was honoured, and he made many friends. It was with the utmost reluctance that the visitor returned home in the summer of 1799. His short stay was an unforgettable experience and he never ceased to speak with longing of the Holy Land.

In an age of Rationalism, the age which produced Moses Mendelssohn (1729-1786) and Solomon Maimon (1754-1800), Rabbi Nachman despised philosophy. Blind faith was preferable, in his view, to subtle dialectics. "Happy is he who knows nothing of their books but who walketh uprightly and feareth retribution." Philosophy fosters doubt and weakens faith. Even Maimonides, the greatest mediaeval philosopher, did not escape censure. "He who looks into the *More* (Maimonides' *Guide to the Perplexed*)," pronounced Rabbi Nachman severely, "loses the divine image of his being."[36]

For the medical profession, too, Rabbi Nachman had nothing but contempt. The sick should rely on God and not on the physician. "Even in a place where there are distinguished doctors, one should neither rely on them nor put one's life in their hands. They are liable to err and can easily do damage which can never be rectified. How much more so the majority of doctors that are to be found in our country, who cannot distinguish their right hand from their left and are veritable killers . . . it is well to avoid them."[37]

Without glorifying poverty, he despised wealth and advocated modesty. Yet these avowed doctrines of 'humility' did not prevent him from indulging in megalomaniac fantasies. He was under the impression that he, and he alone, was the true *Zaddik* and that there was none like him. He alone was fully aware of the greatness of God. "Since the Jews were dispersed from the Holy Land," he declared, "there have been four great periods of learning, and at the centre of each epoch stood a chosen one. There are four chosen teachers, Rabbi Simeon Bar Yochai, Rabbi Isaac Luria, the Besht, and myself."[38] "All *Zaddikim*, after reaching a certain degree of spirituality, remain static; I, however, with the help of God, become another person every day." "In the world to come," he told his disciples, "you may be worthy to understand the hidden meaning that underlies my most casual remark."[39]

The impetuous rabbi had no patience with the conventions and subterfuges of society. His contemporaries did not come up to his standards. Just as Rabbi Jacob Joseph castigated the rabbis, so Rabbi Nachman criticised the *Zaddikim*. "Satan," he said, "found it difficult to lead the world astray, therefore he appointed such men in various places to help him."[40] He was no false prophet to cry "Peace! Peace!" when there was no peace. His criticism was scathing when he felt criticism was called for and he cared nothing for consequences or repercussions. Rabbi Nachman was the great rebel of Hassidism, the revolutionary movement to which Dov Baer, the Maggid, had given respectability. No one could ignore this dynamic descendant of the Besht.

His most powerful opponent was his neighbour, Rabbi Arye Leib (1725-1812), affectionately known as the 'Shpole Zeide' (The Grandfather of Shpole). The Besht attributed to Rabbi Leib Shpole the soul of Rabbi Judah Löw ben Bezalel (Der hohe Rabbi Löw, 1530-1609) of Prague and solemnly declared: "Not for the bodies but for the souls were you sent. There are many outcast souls in this world. It rests with you to strive for them and to save them." The Shpole Zeide was a popular *Zaddik* with many miracles to his credit. He lived to the age of eighty seven (he died on Tishri 6th., 1812) and was well advanced in years by the time Rabbi Nachman came to Shpole. Having known the Besht, Rabbi Phineas of Koretz and the Maggid, Rabbi Arye Leib regarded himself as the 'Lion of the Zaddikim'. Rabbi Nachman's sojourn near Shpole irritated him and these two contrasting personalities clashed again and again. Rabbi Arye Leib regarded Rabbi Nachman as irresponsible and presumptuous, a man who sought to destroy from within what the Gaon failed to destroy from without. "This is not the way a *Zaddik* should conduct himself these days," he said. "Nor is this the manner in which a *Zaddik* should converse."

The mantle of the Vilna Gaon fell on the octogenarian of Shpole. The struggle between the Mitnagdim and the Hassidim was over, and 'civil war' had broken out within the Hassidic movement itself. Its aim had been the 'close fellowship' of Hassid with Hassid but now it was torn by petty jealousies and causeless hatreds. The accusations levelled at the founder of Habad were now hurled at Rabbi Nachman. He was even accused of being an adherent of Shabbetai Zevi and Jacob Frank. Rabbi Levi Isaac of Berdychev intervened in the cause of peace, but without success. Having antagonised his contemporaries, Rabbi Nachman made no attempt to conciliate them. Persecution was the fulfilment of his destiny. "How it is possible," he asked, "that they should not quarrel with me? I walk a path that no one has ever travelled ... I am not really of this world, therefore this world cannot understand me."[41]

In 1802, he settled in Bratslav (Braclaw). There he met

Rabbi Nathan of Nemirov (d. 1830) who became his Boswell. It was Rabbi Nathan who faithfully recorded his aphorisms, his Torah, his stories. Every word was sacred in the eyes of the devoted scholar-scribe, for he believed that "great mysteries are contained in these fables." Rabbi Nachman had high praise for this valuable disciple. "Had I come to Bratslav merely to find him, that in itself would be sufficient." "Nathan! Nathan!" he exclaimed, "You have the power to make my Torah enduring." Rabbi Nachman exerted a powerful influence over his followers. Affectionate and intimate was the relationship between Master and disciples. "How can I ever forget you?" he writes. "Every one of you has a place in my heart ... You all have a share in my Torah." He needed his Hassidim as much as they needed him. "Eat or do not eat, sleep or do not sleep, pray or do not pray; but you must come to me."

When his house was burnt down in 1809, he settled in Uman, infamous site of massacres during the Chmielnicki pogroms. He lived his last three years in the shadow of death. But for him death was merely a change of activity. "After my demise," he told his Hassidim, "whoever will come to my grave and recite ten chapters from the Book of Psalms and contribute to charity on my behalf, even if his sins are many, I will do my utmost to save him." Rabbi Nathan entreated him: "Rabbi, Rabbi, with whom are you leaving us?" The Master comforted his Hassidim. "I am not leaving you. I will be with you always." He died on the third day of Chol Hamoed Succot 1812, and was buried in Uman. No one succeeded him. No one could succeed him. There was no one worthy to take his place.

The inter-movement feuds did not die with the death

of Rabbi Nachman. Left without a leader, his Hassidim, the 'Dead Hassidim' as they were called, were for some time subjected to vindictive persecution.

Rabbi Nachman was the author of various works: *Likutei Tefillot* (collection of prayers), *Likutei Halachot* (collection of *halachot* on the *Shulchan Aruch*), *Sefer ha-Midot* (Treatise on Morals, arranged alphabetically) and *Sippurei Ma'asiyyot* (Stories). To quote his loyal scribe: "Every word written in this holy book is sacred. The stories inscribed here emanated from the mouth of the great *Zaddik* himself." Some thirteen stories and twenty one short tales have been preserved. Among the most famous are: "The Lost Princess," "The Broken Betrothal," "The Cripple," "The King's Son and the Servant's Son," "The Wind that overturned the World," "The Bull and the Ram," "The Prince," "The Spider and the Fly," "The Rabbi's Son," and "The Seven Beggars."

CHAPTER VII

PIONEERS OF POLISH HASSIDISM

During the last quarter of the eighteenth century, the period of the Partitions (1772-1795), over six hundred thousand Jews lived in Poland.

Poland was the *achsanya shel Torah* (the asylum of the Law), and her Yeshivot produced some of the greatest rabbis of Europe. But the masses were unbelievably superstitious and credulous. Conditions were similar to those that prevailed in Volhynia and Podolia in the time of the Besht. Desperately, the people needed the resurrecting force of Hassidism.

One of the earliest pathfinders was Rabbi Israel Haupstein, the Kozienicer Maggid. Israel was born in 1737 to Shabbetai, a poor bookbinder in Apt (Opatow). The Besht himself acted as *sandek*. The child was frail and sickly. He received his early talmudic education under the care of the rabbi of Apt, Dov Berish Katz, grandson of Rabbi Shabbetai Cohen, the *Shach*. Israel's father died in 1761 and the young student settled in Pzysha (near Radom) where he came under the influence of Rabbi Abraham of Pzysha. Like his illustrious namesake, Israel became a teacher. He loved his profession and his pupils loved and revered their teacher.

Rabbi Samuel Horowitz of Ricizival, who settled in Nikolsburg (Southern Moravia) in 1772, became Israel's first guide to Hassidism; once he had tasted 'the forbidden fruit', Israel could no longer delay his journey to Meseritz, then the Zion of the movement. "I studied eight hundred books of the Kabbala and when I arrived at the Maggid of Meseritz, I realised that I had not yet begun to study." The Maggid was enthusiastic about his new disciple. "Blessed be the Holy Name!" he exclaimed, "The Almighty has provided me with a young man who can edit for me the manuscript of Rabbi Isaac Luria's Prayer Book."

Rabbi Israel became closely attached to Rabbi Elimelech of Lishensk (1717-1787), author of *No'am Elimelech*. Despite the teachings of the Besht and the Maggid, Rabbi Elimelech did not entirely discard Lurian practices. He continued to fast and to afflict himself. "My knowledge of the Kabbala," declared Israel, "is superior to that of my teacher Rabbi Elimelech, but, unlike him, I am not able to serve God with such a spirit of self-sacrifice, awe and love." Eventually, Rabbi Israel became *maggid* in Kozienice, a small town north-east of Radom. He was a most eloquent preacher and was superbly equipped for his task. His mastery of the Talmud, his knowledge of the Kabbala, his love of humanity, these made his discourses glow with a fire that inflamed the hearts of all who heard him.

He never forgot the poverty he had suffered as a child and it kept him mindful of his duty to help the poor and needy. The *maggid* once asked one of his wealthy followers: "Tell me, what do you eat every day?" "Rabbi," the miser replied, "I need very little. Bread with salt and water in a measure suffice me." "Your way is not a good one," reproved the *maggid*. "You should eat fatted chickens and drink wine every day. For if you eat well, you will give bread to the poor, but if your menu consists of bread you will begrudge the poor even stones."

Kozienice became a place of pilgrimage and the frail *maggid* won many new adherents to the movement. He wrote halachic, kabbalistic and homiletical works and, like his colleague Rabbi Shneur Zalman, he devoted his life to study. He was on good terms with all his contemporaries, for he was a man without ambition, unassuming and modest in his ways. Rabbi Menachem Mendel of Rymanov once said: "I have heard a heavenly *Bat Kol* (a voice from Heaven) proclaim: 'He who lives in the generation of the *maggid* and does not visit him, will not be worthy to welcome the Messiah!'" Rabbi Israel was deeply concerned with the welfare of Jewry as a whole, and he was one of the twenty four delegates who pleaded with the government for the abolition of the *Shechita* tax. His close contact with the Polish nobility stood him in good stead in his work for Polish Jewry.

The *maggid*, in common with most of his Hassidic contemporaries (with the notable exception of Rabbi Menachem Mendel of Rymanov), sided against Napoleon. Hassidic legend has it that Napoleon's fate was decided not on the battlefields but in the Courts of the Hassidic rabbis. Hassidim even relate that Napoleon came in disguise to the *maggid* to plead with him, but it was of no avail, for the Kozienicer read the verse of Exodus (18. 18) *novol tibbol*, (Thou will surely wear away) as *Nofol tipol* (i.e. Napoleon will fall). Rabbi Israel, lover of God and of Israel, died on the Eve of Succot, 1815.

THE SEER—1745-1815

Early in the nineteenth century, Lublin and Pzysha

73

took the place of Meseritz and Miedzyboz as key centres
of Hassidism. The influence of the Besht, the Maggid and
Rabbi Shneur Zalman had been restricted to the Jews of
Podolia, Lithuania and the Ukraine: now, from Lublin
and Pzysha, Hassidism spread to Polish Jewry. The
father of Polish Hassidism was Rabbi Jacob Isaac, *Ha-
choze*, "The Seer of Lublin". He was born in 1745
and his father Abraham Eliezer was Rabbi in Josefof.
Jacob Isaac was only fifteen years old when the Besht
died and it was due to Rabbi Sussay of Annopal that he
made his way to Meseritz. "A soul had come to us," the
Maggid declared, "that has not made its appearance
since the time of the prophets."

When the *maggid* died in 1772, Jacob Isaac became a
disciple of Rabbi Samuel of Nikolsburg. "When Jacob
Isaac recites the Benedictions," remarked the Rabbi of
Nikolsburg, "the entire Heavenly Court responds
Amen." After a while he journeyed to Rabbi Elimelech
of Lishensk and there the young scholar absorbed
Hassidic lore, together with such fellow-students as
Menachem Mendel of Rymanov and Abraham Joshua
Heschel of Opatow. Rabbi Elimelech even called him
the "Meshiach ben Yosef" and said, "he is as great as I
am."

Hassidim relate that before his death Rabbi Elimelech
bequeathed his body to his disciples. Abraham Joshua
Heschel inherited his mouth (eloquence), Menachem
Mendel of Rymanov acquired the brain, Israel of Kozienice received the heart, Isaac of Kalev was endowed
with his teacher's ear for music and Jacob Isaac his eyes.
The teacher afflicted his body and the disciple followed
his teacher's example. To avoid seeing unseemly things,
the disciple shielded his eyes for seven years until his

sight was seriously affected. But the title 'Seer' came to him because of his inner vision. "When his soul was created, it was given the power to gaze from one end of the world to the other."

In the lifetime of his teacher, Jacob Isaac established a court at Lancut near Lishensk but, doubtless, out of deference to Rabbi Elimelech, in 1794 he moved to Lublin, a city renowned for its scholars and Mitnagdic tradition. Sroka 28, where the Seer established his Beth Hamidrash, soon vied in fame with the *Maharschal's* synagogue. Lublin became not only a centre of Hassidism but also a training ground, a college for Hassidic rabbis. The illustrious Hassidic dynasties of Poland and Galicia, Pzysha, Kotzk, Ger, Worka, Ropczyce, Dynow, all were greatly influenced by the life and lessons of the Seer. His disciples held him in great honour. Rabbi Menachem Mendel of Kotzk called him *Urim Vetumim* (Oracles). Uri of Strelisk, 'The Seraph' (d. 1826), said: "Lublin is *Eretz Yisrael*; the court of the Beth Hamidrash is Jerusalem: the Beth Hamidrash itself is the Temple; the room of the Seer is the Holy of Holies, and the *Shechina* speaks from his mouth." Hassidim believed that when a new Hassid arrived, Rabbi Jacob Isaac instantly took out his soul and cleansed it and restored it to a state of purity, so that its owner became as a new-born babe. He was the author of three works: *Divrei Emet, Zot Zikaron* and *Zikaron Zot*.

On Simchat Torah night (1814), after the *Hakafot* (seven circuits), the Seer was found lying in the Courtyard. He died on Tish' a B'av 1815. His 'mysterious fall' has never been fully explained. "The 'evil power' pursued me," he said.

THE HOLY JEW

The greatest of all the disciples, a giant among giants, was Jacob Isaac, the *Yehudi Hakodosh* (the Holy Jew). Many explanations have been offered for this appellation. Some maintain that it was to differentiate between him and his master the Seer, whose name was identical. Others assert that his soul was that of Mordecai, hero of the Book of Esther. Some believe that it was because Jacob Isaac always gave credit and acknowledgment to any absent authors he quoted in his discourses, or because he would say modestly: "I have heard it from a Jew". Perhaps the truth of the matter is that the title 'Holy Jew' was simply descriptive, for every day of his life the Rabbi strove to be a Jew in the fullest sense of the term.

Jacob Isaac was born in 1765. Asher Rabinowicz, his father, was at one time Rabbi of Grodzysk and Proho-bycz. Like the Besht, the boy studied and prayed in secret, without the knowledge of his parents and teachers. Whenever the Beth Hamidrash was closed and deserted, he would surreptitiously make his way there and spend hours in study and meditation. His first teachers in Kabbala were Arye Leib Heilprin and Meir of Opatow. However, the Yehudi was fond of relating that he was deeply indebted to a smith. One dawn, when the weary scholar was preparing to put aside his books, he heard his neighbour, the smith, still busily hammering away. "If my neighbour can work so assiduously for material things, surely I can work even harder in the ser-vice of the Lord," he reflected. And in the morning, the thought that the smith was already at the anvil drove slumber from his eyes.

While he was living in Opatow (Apt) with his parents-in-law, Jacob Isaac came under the influence of Rabbi Abraham Joshua Heschel (d. 1835), a disciple of both Rabbi Elimelech of Lishensk and Rabbi Yechiel Michal, the *maggid* of Zlotzchow (d. 1781). The Apter was an extraordinary personality. He believed that he had been High Priest in an earlier life. In the Order of Service of the High Priest, recited in the course of the Additional Service on the Day of Atonement, he would change the prescribed text, "And thus did he (i.e. the High Priest) say," to "And thus did I say." *Kavana* was the keynote of his life and his ideal was to serve God without any ulterior motive.

The Yehudi became a teacher in the house of Leibish Frankel Teomim, and it was Rabbi David of Lelov who first took him to the Seer. The Seer was quick to recognise the quality of his new disciple. He prayed: "Let the Lord, the God of the spirits of all flesh, set a man over the congregation who may go out before them and who may come in before them" (Num. 27. 16), and his prayer was answered. He was told that he whose name was identical would teach Torah and worship. Generously, the Master lavished praise upon his pupil. "His soul had already appeared three times; in our patriarch Jacob, in Mordecai, and in Rabbi Jacob ben Meir Tam (1100-1171).

The Yehudi was gifted with outstanding mental faculties that raised him high above the other disciples. He applied to Hassidism the dialectical acumen of talmudic Judaism, and combined a quick wit and a clear brain with a gentle disposition. He was never haughty or overbearing. With patience, and humility, he would expound and explain his precepts to colleagues and disciples.

Many admired him and many were jealous of him. Though the Seer occasionally delegated authority to senior disciples, he could not but resent the influence that the Yehudi was wielding over his associates. Some disciples, such as Menachem Mendel of Kotzk, transferred their allegiance to the Yehudi, who established his own Court in Pzysha. Somehow, the Yehudi managed to arouse the antagonism of the Seer. His frequent visits to Lublin were misconstrued and his every action was misrepresented.

On one occasion, the Seer presented the Yehudi with one of his shirts as a mark of esteem; the gift was valuable in the eyes of the Yehudi. But on the way to the bathhouse a ragged beggar fell at his feet and wept in bitter want. The tender-hearted Yehudi was deeply moved. He had no money to give but he took the shirt which the Seer had given him and handed it to the petitioner. News of this incident was brought to the Seer and he was at first both grieved and indignant at the slight. Hurt by the estrangement, the Yehudi turned to the Seer and pleaded: "Look into my heart! See if there is anger or evil intent." The Seer pierced him with a long and earnest glance. Then he turned away, abashed. "There is no anger, no evil intent in your heart."

When the Yehudi had revealed, according to hidden auguries in the mystical *Book of Raziel*, that he was destined to die after Rosh Hashana, the Master was distraught. "Stay with us. We will keep you alive," he pleaded. But the Yehudi declined. "He could have kept me alive," he said, "but my soul would have suffered for it." The Yehudi died on Tishri 19th., 1813.

The Pzysha doctrine, like Habad, meant a new orientation in Hassidism. In the teachings of the Pzysha school,

78

the Rabbi is no wonder-worker and in any case it is more difficult to be a real Jew than to perform miracles. Study is of the utmost importance. The study of the Gemara (Talmud) and Tosafot purifies the mind. *Kavana* (intention) was the leitmotiv of the Yehudi in prayer, in study, and in every human endeavour. Gestures by themselves are empty and devoid of spiritual content. Only through hard work and sincere desire can one reach the highest pinnacle. The Besht held that there is a spark of Divinity in every Jew. The Yehudi went further: "Every Jew can be like Moses." The Torah (Lev. 19. 11) enjoins: "Ye shall not lie one to another," but it is equally important for a man to be honest with himself. Hassidism has to be alive, dynamic. In Pzysha, prayers were often recited later than the times prescribed in the Codes, for it was thought better to delay the prayers than to pray without proper *Kavana.* Regular hours are suited to normal conditions, but in an emergency, when a state of war exists, unconventional methods are called for. And, for the Hassid, life is a battlefield always, for there can be no armistice between those mortal adversaries, the powers of Good and Evil.

RABBI SIMCHA BUNAM

The Yehudi left three sons, Yerachmiel, Nechemia and Joshua Asher. Yet a majority of the Yehudi's Hassidim appointed Simcha Bunam, the Master's favourite disciple, their spiritual leader.

Simcha Bunam Banehardt was born in 1765 in Wladislaw. His father, Rabbi Zevi, was a popular preacher and the author of learned works. Simcha Bunam received his talmudic education in Nikolsburg under Rabbi Mordecai Benet (1753-1829), Chief Rabbi of Moravia, and his Hassidic training was acquired under Rabbi Moses Leib of Sasov (d. 1829), Rabbi Israel of Kozienice, the Seer and Rabbi David of Lelov. He was employed for a little while by Tamarel Bergson, the 'Doña Gracia' of Hassidism, in her timber business and travelled widely as her representative. The cosmopolitan rabbi visited Danzig and the Leipzig trade fairs. He wore European clothes, spoke Polish and German, frequented the theatre, enjoyed a game of chess. After a few years as a timber merchant, he went back to Lwow and there qualified as a practising chemist. He opened an apothecary shop in Pzysha, where he soon acquired a large clientele. He even supplied medicines to the Napoleonic forces in Russia.

In Pzysha, Simcha Bunam fell under the spell of the Yehudi and the Master held him in high esteem. "The core of my heart", the Yehudi called him, and the "wise Rabbi Bunam" became his spiritual heir. Just as the Maggid had formulated the doctrines of the Besht, so Simcha Bunam interpreted the ideas of the Yehudi. He, too, surrounded himself with a band of hand-picked young men to whom he dedicated his life. Regular periods were set aside for the study of the Talmud and cognate subjects. The study of Kabbala gave way to the study of the mediaeval philosophers. The School of Simcha Bunam concentrated on the *Guide to the Perplexed*, Halevi's *Kuzari*, and the works of the *Maharil* (Judah Löw b. Bezalel 1530-1609) of Prague whom Simcha Bunam regarded as his 'Heavenly Teacher'. His influence over his disciples was tremendous. "He never speaks an idle word," testified one of them. "Whoever sees him will not depart this world without repenting", said another.

Rabbi Simcha Bunam did not lead an isolated life in Pzysha. The troubles of the people were matters that concerned him personally. He opposed the Committee of the Old Covenant and its assimilationist tendencies. Boldly, he told high Russian officials that "it was not the business of the State to interfere in the internal affairs of Jewry. These matters could be safely left in the hands of the Rabbis and the *Zaddikim*. The duty of the State, as far as the Jews were concerned, was to improve their economic position and to alleviate the poverty that prevailed among them."

In his later years, Rabbi Simcha Bunam became blind. He accepted this affliction with the courage and faith and resignation of a man of God. "I prayed to God," he said, "that he should deprive me of my sight in order that I might see the inner light . . . What is good for me to see, I see with the inner light. What is not good to see, I do not wish to see." Rabbi Simcha Bunam held that the truth must permeate every thought, every word and every deed. A man must distinguish clearly between truth and falsehood. And he must, above all, be truthful with himself. Preparation is the basis of prayer and study. A man must first cleanse his heart and mind. It is futile to pray when loaded with sensual desires and worldly thoughts. And it is useless to perform *mitzvot* for ulterior or selfish reasons. This is tantamount to idolatry. A man should be balanced between two scales : one which bears the inscription, "I am dust and ashes", and one which proclaims "the world was created for my sake." In this way, a man can strike the proper balance between overweening pride and false humility.

6

Pzysha Hassidim did not stress congregational prayers nor did they conform to the regular hours of prayer. Commenting on the words of the morning service: "At all times let a man revere God in private as in public, acknowledging the truth in his heart", Simcha Bunam declared: "Only if a man acknowledges the truth and speaks the truth, is he able to 'rise early' and pray at the conventional times laid down by the Sages."

Miracles have no place in Simcha Bunam's philosophy. "Had I known that through miracles I could bring men back to God, I would have planted the trees of Danzig in the streets of Pzysha." He tried to stem the cult of the *Zaddik*. "A fur hat," he said, "and an illustrious father do not make a *Zaddik*." "No doubt Esau, too, wore silk garments and recited Torah at *Shalosh Se'udot*." To be of consequence, a *Zaddik* has to be on a higher spiritual plane than the people. The higher he rises the greater will be his influence on the people below him.

These unconventional sentiments aroused the antagonism of both Mitnagdim and Hassidim. Rabbi Naftali of Ropzyce (1760-1827) called him "dangerous". "I am not saying anything against the Rabbi," explained Naftali. "He is a *Zaddik*, but his way is dangerous to those who follow him. Normally it takes many years to attain piety and fervour. Too quickly his followers achieve the high degree." Simcha Bunam died on Ellul 11th., 1827. As he lay dying, he heard his wife Rebecca weeping: "Why do you weep?" he comforted her. "All my life I have been learning how to die."

RABBI MENDEL OF KOTZK

Rabbi Abraham Moses, son of Rabbi Simcha Bunam, was not the only heir to his father's estate. Many of the Pzysha Hassidim transferred their allegiance to Mendel of Kotzk (Kock).

Rabbi Menachem Mendel Morgenstern was born in 1783, in Goraj, near Lublin. His father, Leibish, was a poor glazier who earned a few inadequate roubles by touring continuously around remote villages. Mendel was an unruly child, ultra-sensitive and highly strung. He was reserved and unsociable. His fellow-students nicknamed him 'Black Mendel', for the brilliant young introvert despised the dull wits around him. His grasp was as quick as lightning and he did not suffer fools gladly. No-one talked his language and no-one understood him. He lived in a world of his own. He regarded as one of his most important teachers the one who instructed him in the alphabet. For teachers of Scripture, Mishna, Talmud and Codes deal with controversial matters; there can be no controversy over the *Aleph Bet*. He studied in the Yeshiva of Rabbi Joseph Hohgelerenter. There, one of his teachers said of him: "Mendel does not make even a gesture without premeditation. His words are deep. His ways are hidden."

At the age of sixteen Mendel made his way to Lublin. When his father reprimanded him sharply for associating with a Hassidic rabbi, Mendel replied: "We read in the Torah (Exodus 15. 2), 'This is my God and I will glorify Him, My father's God and I will exalt him'. These words imply that a spiritual father takes precedence over a physical father." The Seer of Lublin had tried to guide him. "What sort of Rabbi do you seek?" he asked his young pupil. "I seek a Rabbi who is a good Jew, a plain Jew, and who fears God," was the reply.[42] "Your way," the Seer said, "is the way of melancholy. Forsake it, for it has not found favour in my eyes."

Mendel did not change his ways; he changed his Rabbi. With the Yehudi he felt at home. In Pzysha he found a leader after his own heart, a rabbi who scorned the elaborate ritual of the Hassidic court. For the first and only period of his life, he felt that he was understood and that he was no longer alone. With the Yehudi's death, Mendel was left a spiritual orphan and without the Master his life was empty. Hassidim relate that the Yehudi appeared to the bereaved disciple in a dream. "Now that I have been called to the Academy on High, you know not who will be your teacher. Be not disturbed! In the celestial spheres I shall continue to be your guide." Mendel was afraid of no man, living or dead. "I do not want a dead teacher," he rejoined.

Like most of his colleagues, he followed Simcha Bunam at first, but, restless and dissatisfied, he wandered on in self-imposed constant exile, suffering many hardships. He visited Kozienice, Lelov and Szydlowiec. In 1807, he married Glickel Nei of Tomaszow. After the death of Simcha Bunam (1827), he settled in Tomaszow. Two years later, he moved to Kotzk (Kock), where he revived the great tradition of Pzysha.

Mendel hated the stereotyped life that so many of his fellow-rebbes led. He despised the humble Hassidim who begged for his blessings. He disliked the wealthy followers who showered him with money or gifts. "Would to God," he prayed, "that all the Hassidim were Rebbes!" Yet, despite his aloofness, he could not keep the crowds away. The less they were made welcome, the more they came. His very protestations provoked and attracted them. Men made great material sacrifices in order to finance a pilgrimage to Kotzk. And for weeks, for months, in the shadow of the Master they tarried forgetful of family and responsibilities.

Mendel was no rabbi, according to the popular conception of the term. He was not prepared to devote his life to his Hassidism. He was not willing to fritter away his energies on their petty individual problems. His avowed aim was to save the entire House of Israel and to make it a "kingdom of priests and a holy nation." Of what importance were a mere handful of men when the fate of a whole nation was in the balance? Yet, paradoxically, Mendel had a positive horror of crowds, and preferred one discerning disciple to a thousand ignorant enthusiasts. "Would that I had ten white kaftans and no more," he prayed. Mendel was impatient, intolerant and at all times brutally frank. A wealthy follower once asked him: "Do you think that I shall enjoy the world to come?" "You do not enjoy this world for which you have toiled," came the forthright reply. "How can you expect to enjoy the world to come for which you have done nothing?"

Kotzk followed the tradition of Pzysha and attached no importance to miracles. Mendel believed that to transform a Jew into a real Hassid was the greatest miracle of all, and that it was more important and more difficult than the creation of a *Golem*. The God-given injunction to Adam (Gen. 3. 19), "In the sweat of thy brow shalt thou eat bread," applies equally to matters of the spirit. Nothing can be achieved without endeavour. Just as we pray that we may never "need the gifts of flesh and blood," so must we avoid becoming "beggars of the

Almighty." Nor is man to choose the middle way. "All or nothing" was the philosophy of Kotzk, and its pro- tagonist scorned half measures and compromise. Only horses walk in the middle of the road, not men. It is better to be wicked through and through than to be half a *Zaddik*. A perfect gentile is better than an imperfect Jew. Sincerity is of the utmost importance. God's name is Truth. Lip-service and artificialities are hallmarks of the hypocrite. A rabbi is neither a king nor a high priest but an ordinary human being who strives—as every man should strive—to achieve perfection.

Mendel was a dreamer and his dreams soared to the highest spheres. His dreams had strange dimensions and his visions were magnificent, megalomaniacal. "I am the seventh. I am the quintessence of them all. I am the Sabbath. Six generations preceded me; the first was the Besht, the second was the Maggid, the third was Elimel- ech of Lishensk, the fourth was the Seer of Lublin, the fifth was the Yehudi, the sixth was Rabbi Simcha Bunam, and I, Mendel, am the seventh, the Sabbath."[43] "My soul," he said, "is one of those that were created before the destruction of the Temple. I do not belong among the people today. And the reason for my coming into this world is to distinguish between that which is holy and that which is profane."

Rabbi Mendel was severely critical of his Hassidic col- leagues. None of them lived up to his standards. "All the week they do what is right in their own eyes. Comes the Sabbath, they attire themselves in kaftans and fur hats, and, wearing piety like a mantle, they exclaim: 'Come my beloved!' Rabbi Mendel did not necessarily pray at the appointed hours. "In Kotzk," he said: "We have a soul and not a clock. Devout preparation is as important as prayer itself, if it is not more important."

Like the Besht, Mendel was fired by high idealism. Unlike the Besht, Mendel isolated himself from his contemporaries. He regarded himself as a great revivalist, a man with a mission. And the knowledge of his own greatness kept him consciously apart. He did not find in his fellow-men the "image of God". He saw only their faults, their weaknesses. He became an embittered misanthrope. "The whole world is not worth a sigh," was his grim verdict. Nothing could still his spiritual wander-lust. His soul was unsatisfied, his ideals were unattainable, and his life was one long struggle with himself.

One Friday night (Shabbat *Vayishlach*), in 1840, an extraordinary incident took place in the Rabbi's house. It is one of the great unsolved mysteries in the history of Hassidism. Hassidim never discuss the subject. They refer to it as: 'That Friday night'; but their opponents, the Mitnagdim, have no scruples and they tear down the veil. They allege that Mendel cast aside the Kiddush cup that was handed to him by his faithful beadle, Zevi Hirsch of Tomaszow. Touching or extinguishing the Sabbath candles, he cried out: "There is no judgment and there is no judge! Get out of here, you fools. I am neither a Rabbi nor the son of a Rabbi." The following day, as soon as the Sabbath was over, a number of Hassidim, led by Rabbi Mordecai Joseph Lainer of Izbica (1800-1854), author of *Mei Hashiloa*, threw off the yoke of Kotzk. "The *Shechina*", mourned the Hassidim, "has departed from Kotzk." But others remained loyal to their rebbe. Among the faithful were Rabbi Meir of Ger, his son-in-law Rabbi Abraham Bornstein of Sochaczew (author of *Eglei Tal*), Yechiel Meir (1817-1888), the Psalm Jew of Gostynin, and Rabbi Heinoch of Alexander.

For nineteen years, until the day of his death on Shevat 22nd., 1859, the rabbi of Kotzk remained secluded in his study, a voluntary prisoner in a prison without bars. There he prayed, studied, ate and slept. Only once a year, on the day before Passover, did he leave his chamber, that it might be prepared for the festival. He seldom appeared in public. Yet for nearly two decades, Hassidim from all over Poland, outstanding rabbis and scholars among them, continued to make their way to Kotzk. Even some of the 'rebels' returned, for the spell could not easily be broken. Neither his terrifying utterances nor his furious outbursts could keep them away. They clustered in the Beth Hamidrash, studying, meditating, gazing at the closed doors of the Rabbi's room, hoping against hope to behold the countenence of Rabbi Mendel, the stormy petrel of Hassidism. They believed that in his self-imposed isolation he fought a great spiritual battle against evil and hastened the coming of the Messiah.

Mendel destroyed all his manuscripts, but his teachings left a permanent imprint on the Courts of Sochaczew, Ger and Alexander, and on Polish Hassidism in general. His precepts were recorded in the hearts of his disciples, and they were eloquent in his praise. Rabbi Isaac Meir of Ger says: "It is not possible to find a Jew like him. He is as great as the Besht." Rabbi Abraham of Sochaczew goes even further. "From him I have learned wisdom and understanding. He is an Angel of the Lord of Hosts."

CHAPTER VIII

THE THREE GREAT DYNASTIES

Hassidism was born in the second half of the eighteenth century, but the nineteenth century was the Golden Era of the movement. This was the time when almost every East European town and many an East European village had its own Hassidic Court. It is a fact that many a remote little *dorf* (hamlet) in Russia and Poland owes its immortality to the Hassidic Rabbi who lived there and adopted its name as his title. So it was with Belz, Rizhyn, (Ruzhan) and Ger. These small towns produced unique personalities, brilliant luminaries in the Hassidic constellation, who moulded and remade the lives of men, and lent a new brightness, a new richness, a new depth to the Hassidic movement. For more than a hundred years, Ger, Rizhyn, Sadagura and Belz were focal centres, cities of refuge, for Hassidim in Eastern Europe.

Israel Friedmann, founder of the Rizhyn-Sadagura dynasty, was born on Tishri 3rd., 1798 in Prohobycz (Kiev). His father, Rabbi Shalom Shachnah (1771-1802), was the son of Rabbi Abraham 'the Angel' and his mother Havah was the grand-daughter of Rabbi Nachum of Czarnobyl (d. 1795). When Israel was five years old, his father died and the child was brought up by his elder brother, Rabbi Abraham. At thirteen he married Sarah, daughter of the Rosh Yeshiva of Berdychev and later

Rabbi in Butchan. On the death of his brother in 1813, the fifteen year old Israel settled in Rizhyn and there established his Court.

According to legend, the Besht once said, "My soul will return to earth after forty years", and many Hassidim believed that this did in fact happen. For, in many ways, Rabbi Israel of Rizhyn resembled his great namesake. Like the Besht, he had no father to guide and instruct him. Life was his teacher and Nature his inspiration. Like the Besht, he was a man of joy, a man of faith. "He who is oblivious of joy is forgetful of the Almighty." He strongly opposed asceticism of any sort. A man who accustoms himself to fasting and self-mortification does more than afflict his body—he endangers his soul. He was tolerant and kindly, full of love for the children of Israel. "When a Jew takes his *tallit* and *tefillin* and goes to the Synagogue to pray, he is as important today as the Besht and my grandfather the Maggid were in their times."[44]

He had no desire for a following of the élite. His warm humanity embraced the masses. His Court was open to all and the humblest Jew could approach him there without timidity. He regarded himself as a father, welcoming his children home. Their problems were his problems and their peace of mind was precious to him. Learned and unlearned, rich and poor, rubbed shoulders in his house. It was not scholastic discourses or exegetical homilies that attracted people from far and wide, but his personal interest in every individual. He spent a great part of his day listening, comforting, advising, guiding his Hassidim. They knew that they could go to him at any time, consult him on any matter that was troubling them. Each Hassid felt that the rabbi was his friend. His colleagues felt this way about him, too. When Rabbi Joshua Heschel lifted up Israel's girdle and bound it round him, he exclaimed: "Heavens hath honoured me with *gelila*." (the *mitzva* of binding the *Sefer Torah*). Even a rationalist like Rabbi Samson Raphael Hirsch, (1808-1888), the leader of Jewish Orthodoxy in Germany, remarked after visiting him: "It is difficult to perceive how such a man could be born of woman, a man with the light of the *Shechina* shining on his face."[45]

Rabbi Hayyim Halberstamm (1793-1876), prince of the Torah and author of *Divre Hayyim*, visited him also. And this is the reason he gave: "Why was the Temple built on Mount Moriah (where the binding of Isaac took place) and not on Mount Sinai (where the Torah was given to Israel)? Because the place where a Jew is willing to offer his life for the sanctification of God's Name is more important than the place where the Torah was given. The Rizhyner is at all times ready to offer himself for the sanctification of God's Name."

Rizhyn spelt royalty. Rabbi Israel was the Exilarch of Hassidism. He was the first Hassidic rabbi to live in luxury. His home was palatial. His coach was drawn by four horses, his clothes were costly and he employed a vast retinue of servants. He lived like a Polish landowner or a Russian noble rather than like a rabbi. "What can I do?" asked the Rizhyner in justification. "It is not my choice. I am forced from above to take the road of honour and glory and it is impossible for me to deviate from it." He justified the amount of money he spent regularly on his stables in this way. "There are three types of people who normally come to a rabbi: men of piety and renown, *Ba'ale Batim,* and common people. The money that the rabbi receives from the pious he devotes to sacred things, namely, the upkeep of the Synagogue and the purchase of books; the sums derived from the *Ba'ale Batim* are utilised for the day-to-day needs of the household; the money donated by the ordinary people is spent on horses and chariots. These days, the third category is by far the largest, and that is why so much money is available for horses and stables." The Rizhyner was kingly in his manner, too, and his was a dignity that inspired respect.

Rabbi Israel felt a great tenderness for conscripts, young men snatched away from their families, enduring indignities and hardships without redress. When they wept before him because they were forced to desecrate the Sabbath and to contravene the Dietary Laws, the Rizhyner comforted them like a loving father. "When the Messiah comes, it is you who will take precedence over all the *Zaddikim*." Dogma and rigidity had no place in his philosophy. He believed that many—if not all—roads lead to Heaven. Some make their way heavenwards through study, others through prayer, some through teaching, others through learning, some through fasting, others through eating.

In prayer, Rabbi Israel preferred the "still, small voice." When he noticed one of the Hassidim praying loudly and violently, he said to him gently: "My friend, try first the quiet way." He urged his followers to pray at the times prescribed by the Codes.

In 1838, two notorious Jewish informers, Isaac Uksman and Samuel Swartzman, were assassinated. In consequence, many Jews were arrested, Rabbi Israel among them, and taken to Kiev. For twenty two months, he languished in the prisons of Kiev and Kameniec. He accepted his fate with resignation and realism. "Am I better than the head of our family, King David, who suffered persecution at the hands of kings and princes?" he asked. In order to avoid banishment, he acquired an estate in Sadagura near Czernowitz, and then and there the glory of Rizhyn was revived. Rabbi Israel died on Cheshvan 3rd., 1851. "Everyone," he said, "leaves books behind; I leave sons." He also left four daughters. The six sons of Rizhyn established famous Hassidic dynasties.

BELZ

Rabbi Shalom Rokeach, founder of the dynasty of Belz, was born in Brody in 1799. He was a descendant of Eleazer ben Yehuda (1160-1238), author of *Rokeach*, a treatise on ethics and Jewish law. Shalom was brought up by his uncle, Rabbi Issachar Baer, rabbi of Sokal, whose daughter, Malka, he married. She was an extraordinary woman. Anxious that her husband should pursue his studies, she would wake him at night with the words: "Arise, Shalom, to the service of the Creator." For a thousand nights, Shalom kept vigil with the Torah. Mindful of the great debt he owed his wife he applied to her the verse in Genesis (18. 18): "And Melchizedek, King of Salem": i.e. "If Malka (his wife) is a *Zaddeket* (a righteous woman) then Shalom is king."

Shalom visited the leading Hassidic rabbis in turn, Joshua Heschel of Apt, 'The Seraph', Uri of Strelisk (d. 1826), and the *maggid* of Kozienice, but he regarded himself as a disciple of the Seer. "He who knew the Seer realised the heights to which a mortal could attain, and he who knew the Holy Maggid of Kozienice realised how much the love of God meant to a Jew." From time to time, Shalom would leave Kozienice for periodic visits to Lublin. The *maggid* was reluctant to release him. "Stay here," he implored, "and you will see the prophet Elijah." Shalom remained unmoved. "Stay here and you will behold the Patriarchs," the *maggid* promised. But Shalom withstood the temptation. The Seer greeted him warmly. "One who deprives oneself of the privilege of beholding Elijah and the Patriarchs in order to return to his teacher, is indeed a true Hassid."

The Seer predicted that his young disciple would be "the head and leader of thousands of Jews", and honoured him greatly. He once asked Shalom to read the *Megilla* (the Book of Esther). "I have heard this tale related many times," the Seer commented afterwards, "but never as movingly as this." It was on his teacher's advice that Shalom agreed to become a rabbi in Belz, a small town forty miles north of Lemberg.

For forty years, Rabbi Shalom guided followers who came to him from Galicia, Hungary and Poland. Among his disciples were outstanding scholars. From the rabbi of Belz they learnt that the most important things in life were sincerity and simplicity. "In Belz, we discovered that a rabbi can be a rabbi without a *zipice*" (the traditional white garment). They observed Rabbi Shalom at prayer and discovered the meaning of devotion. For he prayed with such intensity that phrases seemed to tumble over one another. His discourses, too, were terse and to the point.

Galicia was the centre of *Haskala* (the "Enlightenment" movement) and Joseph Perl (1774-1839), waged a relentless war against the Hassidim. He accused them of evading the tax on candles, of collecting money for *Eretz Yisrael* and of illegally maintaining Hassidic synagogues and printing Hassidic literature. Conversely, the high incidence of apostasy among the *Maskilim* convinced Rabbi Shalom that *Haskala* represented a mortal threat to traditional Judaism and he was not prepared to meet the enemy half way. There is no half way house, no No-Man's Land, in Judaism. "In the Codes, the *Shulchan Aruch, Orach Hayyim* (The Way of Life), *Yore De'a* (Teacher of Knowledge), *Even ha-Ezer* (The Stone of Help), which deal with relations between God and man, the term 'compromise' is not to be found. Only in the *Hoshen Mishpat* (The Breastplate of Judgement) which deals with monetary matters does the word occur."

Rabbi Shalom was a fighter by nature. From boyhood onwards, he had excluded from his life all activities that might distract him from his studies and his struggle for spiritual self-betterment. Now he devoted himself with all his habitual thoroughness and perseverance to the fight against the *Maskilim*. And he regarded the slightest deviation from the path of orthodoxy as rank heresy. He laid great stress on traditional education. "Days are coming," he said, "when to rear a son in the Torah and in the fear of God will be as hard to accomplish as the binding of Isaac." To the very end (he died on Elul 27th., 1855), he fought against *Haskala* and its influence.

Rabbi Joshua Rokeach (1825-1894), fifth and youngest son of Rabbi Shalom, succeeded his father. He, too, was a great halachic authority. He was also the first Hassidic rabbi to engage actively in politics. To counteract the activities of the "Shomer Yisrael" association and their organ *Israelit,* which was established in 1866 to disseminate the doctrines of the Enlightenment, Rabbi Joshua formed the *Machzikei Hadat* in 1878, opening branches in many cities, and he issued two weekly papers of his own, *Machzikei Hadat* and *Kol Machzikei Hadat*. In the face of danger, there is no room for disunity and Rabbi Joshua enlisted the active co-operation of the Mitnagdim. Rabbi Moses Simeon Sofer (Schreiber) 1815-1871, son of the Chatam Sofer, became titular head of the movement. It was largely due to the exertions of the Belzer that Rabbi Simeon was elected a member of the Austrian Parliament in 1879.

Rabbi Issachar Dov (1854-1927), second son of Rabbi Joshua, was also a great fighter for orthodox Judaism. When it was decreed that rabbis must take state examinations, he pleaded eloquently with the Governor of Lwow: "If your excellency wished to construct railways, would he not call in engineering experts to guide and advise? Surely in such a matter he would not consult shoemakers. Similarly, in matters affecting the welfare and status of the rabbinate, only rabbis should be consulted."

At the outbreak of the First World War, he left Belz and settled first in Ratzfeld (1914-18), and then in Munkacz (1918-21). In 1925 he returned to Belz. He employed a personal attendant, Jacob the Maggid, whose sole and singular duty was to admonish and rebuke his master at regular intervals. When they were dining together one day, Jacob the Maggid remarked "The Rabbi is seated. He eats and drinks unmindful of the people in the town who have no food." Rabbi Issachar Dov immediately left the table in order to collect money for the needy. He died on Cheshvan 24th., 1927, mourned by Hassidim in many countries.

GER

"Everything needs *mazzel*, even a *Sefer Torah* in the Ark," runs an old adage which can well be applied to Ger (Gora kalwaria). The little townlet on the Vistula near Warsaw was fortunate enough to become the Jerusalem of one of the greatest of the Hassidic dynasties.

Isaac Meir Rothenburg (Alter), better known as the *Hiddushe Harim*, was born in Magnishev where his father Israel was rabbi. Among his ancestors were Rabbi Meir ben Baruch of Rothenburg (ca. 1215-1293), Rabbi Joel Serkes, Rabbi Jonathan Eybeschutz and Rabbi Nathan Shapira. Isaac Meir, the Gaon of Hassidism, was heir to the scholarly attainments of his forefathers. At nine, he became engaged to Feigele, daughter of the wealthy Moses Halfan Lipshitz, and the wedding took place in Warsaw in 1811. After a short stay in Kozienice, he settled in Warsaw which was steadily developing into a great Jewish centre. The small Yeshiva of the 'Illui of Warsaw' attracted young men of exceptional talent.

The youthful Isaac Meir was of a retiring disposition. He had no desire for high office, and declined many honours within his reach. The rabbinical authorities of Warsaw recognised the qualities of the dedicated student and encouraged him in his studies. In 1842, he was one of the signatories to a manifesto urging Jews to settle on the land. "Not only is there no trace of prohibition found in the Talmud ... on the contrary, we find in the Talmud that many of the saintly *Amoraim* actually owned estates, fields and vineyards."

He visited the Seer, the *maggid* of Kozienice and his son Rabbi Moses Eliakim Briah, (d. 1828). But when the latter kissed him, he exclaimed: "I do not want a rabbi

97

who embraces but one who chastises and rebukes." He greatly revered the Holy Jew of Pzysha. "When the Yehudi smokes his pipe, his thoughts are the very same thoughts that were in the mind of the High Priest officiating in the Holy of Holies." But circumstances frustrated him and, to his lifelong regret, he never visited the Holy Jew.

In Rabbi Simcha Bunam, spiritual heir to the Yehudi, Issac Meir found solace for his soul, and he visited Rabbi Simcha Bunam no less than seventeen times. "Just as the Torah was given on Mount Sinai with thunder and lightning, so we receive the Torah in Pzysha every day." The teacher, too, valued highly his learned disciple. "Had he lived in the time of the *Tannaim*," Rabbi Bunam said, "he would have been a *Tanna*."

When Rabbi Simcha Bunam died, Isaac Meir became a follower of Kotzk and later the two families were allied in marriage. In 1837, his sister-in-law married Rabbi Mendel and in 1844 his granddaughter (daughter of Abraham Mordecai) married Rabbi Benjamin, son of Rabbi Mendel. Isaac Meir's enthusiasm for Rabbi Mendel never waned. In the depths of winter, he took his grandchildren to Kotzk. "It is all worth while in order that they should behold a true Jew."

The Polish Insurrection of 1831 reduced his father-in-law to poverty. Isaac Meir tried hard to make a living. He made *talleisim*, sold books, turned printer. It was not until 1852 that he was officially appointed *Dayan* at Warsaw with a fixed salary.

Rabbi Mendel of Kotzk died in 1859 and Isaac Meir became a Hassidic Rebbe. "Rabbi Bunam," he said, "led with love, while Kotzk led with fear. I shall lead with Torah." He had a high conception of his mission. "I am not a Rebbe. I do not want money. I do not want honour. All I want is to spend my years bringing the children of Israel nearer to their father in Heaven."[46] The teachings of Pzysha and Kotzk were not forgotten. In Ger, too, there was no emphasis on miracles and no acceptance of *pidyonot* (money gifts). The Rebbe was no substitute for personal endeavour. "Believe me," Rabbi Isaac Meir once exclaimed to his Hassidim, "if the people who come here will not exert themselves, not even the *Zaddikim* of the generation will be able to help them." "There is an old proverb: 'If you cannot cross over, you do not cross over,' but I say that the more impossible a task seems, the harder one should strive to accomplish it." Torah is the source of life. When a Hassid once complained that he was without a friend, the Rabbi retorted, "Surely you have a *Gemara* in your house?"

Rabbi Isaac Meir was uncompromising in his struggle against compulsory assimilation. He opposed the *ukase* of May 1st. 1850 prohibiting the wearing of a distinctive Jewish form of dress.[47] He was equally adamant in his opposition to any change in the Jewish educational system. When Sir Moses Montefiore (1784-1885) was in Warsaw (May 13th.-23rd., 1846), Rabbi Isaac Meir, together with Rabbi Isaac of Worki (Warka), called upon him at the Angelsky on May 22nd. and tried to enlist his support. "The same day," writes Dr. Louis Loewe, "a deputation of the pre-eminently conservative class of the Hebrew community of Hassidim paid us a visit. They wore hats, according to European fashion, instead of the Polish *czapka* or the *mycka* which is similar to that of the Circassian. They were headed by Mr. Posener, who had done much for the promotion of industry in Poland, and his son."[48]

This was not the only meeting. On May 20th, Sir Moses had written: "There is much to be done in Poland I have already received the promise of many of the Hassidim to change their fur caps for hats and to adopt the German costume generally. I think this change will have a happy effect on their position, and be the means of producing a good feeling between their fellow subjects and themselves. I have received the assurance of many that they would willingly engage themselves in agriculture if they could procure land: and his Highness the Viceroy is desirous that they should do so."[49]

Rabbi Isaac Meir died on Adar 23rd., 1866. Among his many published works are *Hiddushe Harim* on talmudical tractates, *Teshuvat Harim* (Responsa) on Codes, and *Hiddushe Harim* on *Hoshen Mishpat*.

Rabbi Isaac Meir's personal life was beset by tragedies. He had thirteen children and outlived them all. He was succeeded by his grandson Yehuda Leib, son of Abraham Mordecai (d. 1855). Yehuda Leib was born in Warsaw in 1847. To his grandfather's great joy, the lad was indefatigable in his study of the Torah. "Come," Rabbi Isaac Meir used to say "and see how my grandson studies Torah for its own sake." However, Yehuda Leib had no desire to become a Rebbe and for a time attached himself to Rabbi Heinoch of Alexander. When Rabbi Heinoch died, Yehuda Leib assumed the leadership of the Gerer Hassidim. Like his grandfather, he would not accept gifts. He believed in the dignity of labour and held that a rabbi who accepts the gifts of flesh and blood automatically forfeits his independence. He advised his followers not to "make the Torah a crown with which to aggrandise oneself, nor a spade with which to dig." He was no respecter of wealth and in his

Court scholarship and piety took precedence over wealth.

Rabbi Yehuda Leib participated in the Conference convened in 1888 by the rabbi of Grodzysk to seek out ways and means of safeguarding the traditional Jewish educational system, and he volunteered to collect one hundred thousand roubles for this purpose. During the Russo-Japanese war, he did all he could to help Jewish conscripts who wrote to him from the battlefields of Manchuria. He died on Shevat 5th., 1905. His works, the *Sefat Emet* (Lips of Truth) on the Pentateuch and *Likutei Emet,* are a significant contribution to Hassidic literature. During the lifetime of the *Sefat Emet,* the empire of Ger grew great and powerful.

Rabbi Abraham Mordecai (1866-1943) son of Rabbi Yehuda Leib, made important innovations. In 1906, he instituted early morning services, a bold departure from Pzysha and Kotzk. He drew young people into Hassidism. He participated actively in the work of the Agudah and attended the Agudist Conferences of 1923, 1929 and 1937. He died in Jerusalem on Shavuot, 1948. Dr. Isaac Herzog (1888-1959), then Chief Rabbi of the Holy Land, pronounced these words in fitting eulogy: "On Shavuot the Torah was given and on Shavuot the Torah was taken away."

CHAPTER IX

THE ROLE OF THE HASSIDA

Popular misconception puts the Hassidic woman firmly in her place—the kitchen and the nursery— assigning to her the sole function of producing and serving an ever-increasing family. This is a falsification of the facts. The Hassida, as she was called, occupied an honourable and honoured position.[50] Hassidism needed and accepted her wholehearted support. Often it was the wife who 'converted' the husband. For Hassidism had a strong appeal to women. They reacted with sensitivity and appreciation to the basic principles of the movement—the warm emotionalism, the joyful affirmation of life, the stress on self-fulfilment, the endowment of mundane day-to-day tasks with noble meaning. So Hassidism fired the imagination of the women and they read Hassidic anecdotes (printed in Yiddish) as avidly as their twentieth century counterparts devour romantic novelettes.

The Besht remembered with deep gratitude the devotion of his own wife Hannah. Despite the violent opposition of her brothers, Hannah had married Israel as a poor and obscure peasant (as the hidden master then appeared) and their abiding love had weathered many hardships. Israel loved her deeply and when she died he did not remarry. "Heaven," he said, "has departed with her." In his great sorrow he cried, "I thought that a storm would sweep me up to Heaven like the prophet Elijah, but now that I am only half a body, that is no longer possible." In his last Testament, *Tzavaat ha-Ribash* he stresses the *Mitzva* of loving and honouring a wife. The Besht had also the greatest affection for his daughter Adel.

When the Besht visited Satanov, he perceived a great spiritual light and found that this radiance emanated from a woman. "Shame on you!" he rebuked the leaders of the community. "Through a woman have I seen light". He considered that the prayers of women carried great power and in support related the following anecdote: A certain community had once proclaimed a public fast in order to ward off a great calamity that threatened the people. The whole community, men and women, young and old, assembled in the synagogue. The rabbi wept before the Ark, trembling with terror, and he prayed with solemnity and single-mindedness. Yet the Gates of Heaven were forced and the floodgates of Mercy loosened by the cry from the heart of an ordinary woman, a humble mother in Israel. "Master of the Universe!" she pleaded. "Thou art a merciful father. Thy children are pouring out their hearts to Thee. I am a mother of five children and when I hear their cry, my heart goes out to them. Heavenly Father, Thou hast many children. Even if Thy heart were made of stone, it should melt at the agonising cry of Thy children. O God, listen to them and save them."

Husbands were not always gratified by the spiritual prowess of their wives. Yet when Jonah Spradlaver complained to the Besht of his Yante's strange behaviour, the Master reassured him. "She has seeing eyes and hearing ears," he announced enigmatically, and added the title "prophetess" to her name.

Hassidic writers tried increasingly to raise the prestige of women in Jewish life. Hassidic Rabbis constantly endeavoured to improve their status. The wife of one of his opponents met the Berdychever Rabbi one day in the street and poured a pail of water over his head. Rabbi Levi Isaac went to the Synagogue and prayed: "O Lord, God of Israel, do not punish the good woman. She must have done this at her husband's command, and she is therefore to be commended as a loyal wife."

To lighten the burden of the widow was a great *Mitzva*, and the Hassidic rabbis did not stand on their dignity when they were performing it. The famous Zanzer rabbi, Hayyim Halberstamm (1793-1876), author of *Divre Hayyim*, was once walking through the marketplace when he noticed a widow behind her fruit stall bitterly bewailing the lack of customers. Without further ado, Rabbi Hayyim took her place at the stand and shouted: "Buy fine apples, a dozen a gulden!" The news that the *Zaddik* had turned salesman spread through the market and all the people rushed to buy from the Holy Man. The poor widow made a fine profit that day.

Not since the Bible times that brought forth the 'Four Matriarchs' and the 'Seven Prophetesses', has Jewry produced women as outstanding as those who emerged in the heyday of Hassidism. Rabbi Leib, son of Sarah (1710-1791) was the only Hassidic personality whose name was always associated with that of his mother. Sarah, a woman of rare beauty, had married an elderly scholar in order to escape the unwelcome attentions of the squire's son. Rabbi Leib Sarah is the centre of more stories than any other *Zaddik* save the Besht. He is the

Elijah of the Hassidic leaders, the wandering rabbi, travelling from place to place, helping, rescuing and redeeming fellow-Jews.

Feige, daughter of Adel and mother of Rabbi Nachman of Bratzlav was said to be endowed with "divine spirit". It was her influence, rather than that of her husband, Rabbi Simcha, that inspired her illustrious son.

Like Rashi's daughter, Merish, daughter of Rabbi Elimelech of Lishensk (1717-1787), was renowned for her scholarship. Hassidim would flock to hear her learned discourses and to receive her blessings. Freida, daughter of Rabbi Shneur Zalman, was highly honoured among Habad Hassidim. She transmitted many of her father's sayings to her brother Rabbi Dov Baer (1773-1827). She also left behind a number of remarkable manuscripts dealing with a variety of subjects.

Even the study of Kabbala did not satisfy the spiritual aspirations of certain Hassidic women. Perele, daughter of Rabbi Israel of Kozienice and wife of Rabbi Ezra Zelig, rabbi of Magnewishuv, wore *tzitzit* (ritual fringes), fasted on Mondays and Thursdays, and received petitions from her followers. She lived a life of poverty. All the money that she received from the Hassidim was promptly distributed among the poor. "The *Shechina* rests upon her," acknowledged Rabbi Elimelech of Lishensk, and her own father urged his Hassidim to visit her.

Rachel, daughter of Rabbi Abraham Joshua Heschel of Apt (1745-1825), was equally renowned. Her father was an ardent believer in her powers. "She has a holy spark," he said. She accompanied him on his many journeys and he consulted her constantly. Most Apter Hassidim paid court to the daughter as well as to the father. The Hassidim fervently believed that she, too, could accomplish great things.

Malka, wife of Rabbi Shalom of Belz (1845-1779), was famous for her piety. "The rabbi of Belz and his wife," it was said, "were like Adam and Eve before they sinned in the Garden of Eden." He would consult her on almost every problem and his example was followed by his Hassidim. On one occasion a man complained to her of a pain in his leg. She advised him to light a candle every day in the Synagogue. He did so, and made a complete recovery. When Rabbi Shalom asked her how she had wrought the miracle, she replied, "It is written in Psalms (119. 105) "Thy word is a lamp unto my feet . . ."

Like mother, like daughter. Eidele, her daughter, married Rabbi Isaac Rubin, a descendant of Rabbi Naftali Zvi of Ropsyce. Despite his illustrious ancestry, Rabbi Isaac Rubin was reluctant to become a rabbi. No such reluctance was displayed by his wife. She more then made up for his hesitancy. She delivered discourses, distributed *shirayim* and conducted herself as a fully-fledged rabbi. Her father, Rabbi Shalom, said of her : "All Eidele needs is a rabbi's hat."

Sarah, daughter of Rabbi Joshua Heschel Teumim Frankel, made a name for herself among the Hassidim. She was born in 1838 in Tarnapol. Her father died when she was only three months old. Rabbi Josele, the 'Good Jew of Neustadt', married her to his grandson Rabbi Hayyim Samuel Horwitz-Strenfeld. After her husband's death (Shevat 18th., 1916), she conducted herself like a Hassidic Rebbe. She was famous for her apt sayings and stories. A regular *ma'amadot* was instituted for her up-keep. Even rabbis and rebbes visited her and solicited her blessings. The monies she received from the Hassidim were distributed among the poor. She fasted regularly and mortified her body, but her asceticism did not affect her longevity. She died in 1937, at the age of ninety-nine.

The daughter of Rabbi Abraham of Trisk (1806-1889), Malkale, popularly known among the Hassidim as 'Malkale the Triskerin', was likewise a fully-fledged rabbi. She conducted *tish* (public meals) distributed *shirayim*, and twice every day received petitions from Hassidim. She insisted on being present in her father's room when the Hassidim visited the *maggid*.

Another celebrated woman-rabbi was Hannah Havah, daughter of Rabbi Mordecai Twersky (1770-1837) of Czarnobyl. Her father testified that she was endowed "with the Holy spirit from the womb and from birth." He deemed her equal in piety to his sons, 'the eight candles of the Menorah'. Her aphorisms and parables spread her fame throughout Poland. She ministered to men, but her main concern was with her own sex. She dealt tenderly and tirelessly with the women who flocked to her for guidance. She emphasized the importance of correct and careful education, and extolled the virtue of Charity.

Most famous of all the Hassidic women was Hannah Rachel (1805-1892), the only daughter of Monesh Werbemacher, who became known as the Maid of Ludomir. The limited education that was provided for girls did not satisfy Hannah Rachel. She studied the Midrash, the Aggada and many books of *musar*. She was exceptionally sensitive. Her prayers were full of devotion and true passion. She was betrothed at an early age; but the betrothal brought her little happiness. She became very moody, alternating between fits of exultation and periods of prolonged melancholy and depression. Affectionate and warmhearted by nature, she was forced to live a lonely and friendless existence. There was no-one to share her thoughts. Her only place of comfort was the grave of her mother. There she poured out all her longings and inner desires.

On one of her regular visits to the cemetery, she fell fast asleep at the graveside. When she awoke, it was midnight and the world was dark. The weird surroundings of the deserted 'House of Life' filled her with terror. Half dazed, she began to run and stumbled into one of the half-filled graves. Fear and horror left a terrible imprint on her already frail constitution. She became very ill and hovered between life and death. On recovering from her dangerous illness, she made a startling announcement: "Father, I have just been in the Heavenly Court and there I received a new and sublime soul." Indeed the new Hannah Rachel was a different person. She donned *tzitzit*, wrapped herself in a *tallit* and, like Michal, daughter of King Saul, she put on *tefillin*. When her father died, she recited *Kaddish* and later broke off her engagement.

Financially well provided for by her father, she spent her time in pious meditation. A synagogue was built with an adjoining apartment for her. Every Sabbath at *Shalosh Se'udot* the door of her room would be opened. Heard, but unseen, the Maid of Ludomir would deliver Hassidic discourses. Among the many who crowded round her were scholars and even rabbis; and they were known as the "Hassidim of the Maid of Ludomir". Finally at the age of forty, she succumbed to the persuasive tongue of the Czarnobiler Rabbi and agreed to marry a talmudical scholar. Her influence waned after the marriage and she emigrated to the Holy Land.

The change of country was stimulating. She formed a close association with a Kabbalist and both were determined to work for the speedy advent of the Messiah. After prolonged and elaborate preparations, a time and place were fixed for the enactment of the great drama. The Maid of Ludomir arrived punctually at the appointed cave outside Jerusalem and anxiously awaited her associate. She was destined to disappointment. Her Kabbalist collaborator failed to honour the appointment. The failure of the Kabbalist to turn up was no accident. Like the Maid, he had set out on his great mission but he had been detained by a venerable sage who simply would not release him. The stranger was none other than the ubiquitous prophet, Elijah, in disguise. The time for the advent of the Messiah was not yet nigh.

The women on the Hassidic 'Roll of Honour' who were 'rabbis' and 'wonder workers', students of the Kabbala and learned Talmudists, were of course exceptions. But even the great number of Hassidic women who were themselves unlearned were often largely responsible for the erudition of their husbands and sons. Through the hard work and suffering of these devoted wives, the rabbis were enabled to devote themselves exclusively to matters of the mind and the soul. Feige, wife of Rabbi Isaac Meir of Ger, was a draper, and Yocheved, wife of Rabbi Yehuda Leib of Ger became a sugar-merchant. The wife of Rabbi Jacob of Radzimin turned travelling pedlar, wandering from village to village with her wares. Perele, wife of Rabbi Nathan David of Szydlowiec, supervised an estate, and Hannah Deborah, wife of Rabbi Zadok Cohen of Lublin, dealt in clothes.

A great part was played in Hassidic life by Tamarel Ahitkover Bergson, wife of Baer Smulewitch Zanenberg and ancestress of the French philosopher Henri Bergson. What Beatrice de Luna (Gracia Méndez), 1510-1569, did for the Sephardim in the sixteenth century, Tamarel did for the Hassidim in the nineteenth century. A number of Hassidic rebbes worked for her and she was a devoted Hassida of Rabbi Isaac of Worka, Rabbi Mendel of Kotzk and Rabbi Isaac Meir of Ger. Her generosity and kindliness were proverbial and her mission in life was to help fellow Hassidim.

The Hassidim were unyielding in their opposition to *Haskala*. No secular subject was allowed to penetrate the walls of the Yeshiva. No Yeshiva student dared to read *Haskala* literature openly. The works of Judah Leib Gordon (1830-1892), Abraham Mapu (1808-1867) or Shalom Jacob Abramowitsch (1835-1917), *Ahavat Zion* (the Love of Zion) and *Ayit Tsavua* (the Painted Hawk) were perused in secret. But Hassidic fathers were more tolerant in their attitude towards their daughters. Though Glückel of Hameln (1646-1724) speaks of *cheder* education for girls, this is certainly not representative of life in Poland, where the intellectual thirst of the women had to be satisfied with the *Ze'ena Ure'ena* by Rabbi Jacob b. Isaac Askhenazi of Janov (sixteenth century) and folk tales.

In the beginning of the twentieth century and especially after the First World War, many Hassidic parents encouraged their daughters to study. Some even prided themselves on the intellectual attainments of their eager and intelligent young women. In the small towns of Poland, private tutors were in great demand. Music, Polish and French were the favourite subjects. In the larger towns, there were Jewish schools, such as the *Tarbut* (Hebrew) and *Zisho* (Central Jewish School Society where Yiddish was used) established by the Hechalutz and Hashomer Hatzair movements, but these were taboo to Hassidic circles. Yet many frequented the gentile *gymnasium* and some even completed the curriculum of 'eight classes'.

Secular education stood the women in good stead. They were often the breadwinners and were able to converse with their gentile customers. But fathers soon repented of their 'worldliness'. Not infrequently the peace and harmony of the Hassidic home was shattered by the conflict between emancipated daughter and 'old-fashioned' father. Many refused to acquiesce in the paternal choice of husband. They began to despise both the *shadchan* and the *sheitel*. They looked down on the *Yeshiva bachur* and regarded him as unworldly. New knowledge gave them new ideas. Dissatisfaction led to open rebellion and many young women eloped with their lovers.

The social aspect, too, could not be ignored. In the words of Sarah Schenierer: "And as we pass through the Elul days, the trains which run to the little *shtedlech* (towns) where the Rabbis lived are crowded. Thousands of Hassidim are on their way to them to spend the *Yomim Noraim* (High Holidays) with the rabbi. Every day sees new crowds of old men and young men in the Hassidic garb eager to secure a place in the train, eager to spend the holiest days in the year in the atmosphere of their Rebbe, to be able to extract from it as much holiness as possible. Fathers and sons travel; and those who can afford it make this journey several times a year. Thus they are drawn to Ger, to Belz and to Alexander, to

111

Bobov, to all those places that had been made citadels of concentrated religious life, dominated by the leading figures of a Rabbi's personality. And we stay at home, the wives and the daughters and the little ones. We have an empty *Yom Tov*. It is bare of Jewish intellectual concentration. The women have never learned anything about the spiritual content that is concentrated within a Jewish festival. The mother goes to *Shool*. The Service rings faintly into the fenced and boarded-off women's galleries. There is much crying by the elderly women. The young girls look on them as being of a different century."[51]

The social and educational problems were partially solved by the Beth Jacob school system sponsored by the Agudah. In 1917, Sarah Schenierer opened the first school in her native town, Cracow, with thirty pupils. The progress of the movement was phenomenal. Within a decade there were eighty seven schools throughout Poland with ten thousand nine hundred and five pupils. Hassidic rabbis were wholehearted in their support and the Rabbi of Ger (Abraham Mordecai Alter) gave it his blessing. "It is a sacred duty to work nowadays for the Beth Jacob Movement," he wrote. At the beginning of the Second World War, there were thirty eight thousand girls attending two hundred and fifty three Beth Jacob Schools. The future mothers of Israel were educated in the true traditional spirit of the Torah and were equipped with a sound all-round schooling.

It is clear that in Hassidism the women were neither 'voiceless' nor 'suppressed'. Hassidic writers and rabbis acknowledged openly and appreciatively the vital rôle of women in Jewish life. They consciously raised her prestige and accorded her the greatest respect. It did not matter that she has neither the time nor the opportunity for esoteric study or spiritual achievement. Hassidism gave a new meaning and nobility to the most menial task, to the most mundane drudgery of day-to-day life, and granted its women full equality in this world and in the world to come.

8

CHAPTER X

THE HASSIDIC WAY OF LIFE

Hassidism is one of the 'martyr movements' of history. Like religious sects throughout the ages, Hassidim were persecuted and vilified. Their principles were distorted and their practices maligned. Learned Talmudists put aside the calm deliberation that cloaked their every utterance; precipitately, they condemned the movement and excommunicated its followers. In this instance, the protagonists of *Jüdische Wissenschaft* sided with their bitter opponents the Mitnagdim, and were equally irrational and unenlightened in their condemnation. Heinrich Graetz (1817-1891) illuminates many an obscure period in his monumental *History of the Jews,* but he was plainly groping in the dark when he dealt with the movement that was making such headway in his own lifetime. Graetz could revive the dead, but could not assess the living. According to him, "the new sect, a daughter of darkness, was born in gloom and even today proceeds stealthily on its mysterious way."[52] Hassidism had to wait until the twentieth century to receive a realistic valuation. Many historians and writers of this century—among them Simon Dubnow, Martin Buber, S. A. Horodezky, Gershon G. Scholem, Eliezer Steinmann and Hillel Zeitlin—entered the 'Pardes', the

Garden of Hassidism, and assigned the Movement an honourable position in the chronicle of religious revivals.

Although Hassidism had its philosophers, there was no yawning chasm between theory and practice. The life of the Hassid was always regarded as the best exposition of Hassidism. The movement never claimed originality. Its impact on Eastern European Jewry was cataclysmic, but its contents were traditional. For the Besht was a revivalist rather than a revolutionary. He wanted to re-vitalise the Jewish religion and the Jewish people. He had no desire to remake or to remodel. He wanted to remove the pebbles, to make the crooked straight and the rough places smooth. Unlike the Essenes, the Hassi-dim did not subscribe to ascetic and communistic prin-ciples. They did not approve of detachment from the turmoil of the material world; nor did they have any-thing in common with the eighth century Karaites (Readers of the Scripture) who abrogated Rabbinic auth-ority. The Besht laid foundations upon which many superstructures were erected. The Hassidic sky was com-posed of many planets, each set in its appointed place, each revolving round its own orbit, each con-tributing to the brilliant light that floodlit the Jewish world. There were marked differences in outlook be-tween the rabbis of Rizhyn, and Kotzk, Sochaczew and Sadagura, yet all were united in common fellowship. This universal fellowship is one of the great achieve-ments of Hassidism. Under the wings of the Besht, all can shelter, the rich and the poor, the scholar and the un-learned alike. But though Hassidism uplifts the poor, it does not degrade the wealthy. It simply eliminates the barriers between man and man, and between man and his Maker. It recognises no aristocracy, neither the aristocracy of wealth, nor the aristocracy of intellect. All are Children of the Living God. All men are equal, and no man is more equal than his neighbour. Hassidism translates the phrase: 'All Israel are united in fellowship', into every phase of human relationship.

It is as difficult to define a Hassid as it is to define a Jew. Hassidism has no 'articles of faith', nor does it demand adherence to a formal code. A Hassid is recognised not by the belief he holds but by the life he leads. Faith in the *Zaddik*, joy, humility, devotion (*kavana*) and enthusiasm (*hitlahavut*), these are the signposts to the Hassidic way of life. Hassidism gives a sense of importance to everything and to everyone. No action is insignificant, no thought is trivial. Every Jew is a co-worker of the Almighty in the work of creation. Every Jew, however humble, can help himself—and others. The true Hassid avoids soul-destroying egotism. He cultivates sensitivity, kindliness, generosity. Above all he avoids pride, the attribute of Satan.

The term 'Hassid' is not an eighteenth century creation. It is used in the Bible to connote a man of piety and Godliness. It is even applied to the Deity. "The Lord is righteous in all His ways and pious (*Hassid*) in all His works," sings the Psalmist (Psalm 145. 17). The Hassidim "exult in glory, they sing for joy upon their beds. They have the high praises of God in their mouths and a two-edged sword in their hands" (Psalm 149. 5).

The *Zaddik* did not originate with the Besht. "Noah was in his generation a man righteous (*Zaddik*) and whole-hearted" (Gen. 6, 9). "The *Zaddik*," says the prophet Habakkuk (2, 4), "shall live by his faith." The Book of Psalms lists the attributes of the *Zaddik* and the Book of Job depicts his trials and sufferings. Even God is

116

described as *Zaddik*: "A *Zaddik* and a Righteous One is He" (Deut. 32. 14). In talmudic literature, the power of the righteous can be summed up in the saying: "God decrees and the Righteous annuls" (*Moed Katan*, 16b). Hassidism developed these concepts in everyday life and produced a type of leader who is unique in the Jewish religious hierarchy. He is called *Zaddik, Rebbe, Giter Yid* (Good Jew). He is no official of the *Kahal*. Nor is he elected by the community. Unlike the Rabbi (*Rav*) he requires no ordination, and unlike the priest (*Cohen*) his is not necessarily an hereditary office. His authority comes from the people, and in this way he is closer to the prophet than the priest. The *Zaddik* was not self-sufficient. He looked down to his followers for inspiration, just as they looked up to him for guidance. Though he reached for the skies, he never forgot his earthly duties.

Many were reluctant to become rabbis. The Maggid stressed the heavy responsibilities of the leader. "His heart is flooded with the life-blood of others and weighed down with the sorrows of his people." "What is my transgression," he complained, "that I have become renowned?" The Rabbi's self-imposed duties were onerous. Before the birth of Rabbi Levi Isaac of Berdychev—runs the legend—Satan writhed in anguish. He feared that the saint would perfect and purify the House of Israel. But his fears were allayed. He was assured that Levi Isaac would become a Rebbe and would be so enmeshed in communal matters that Satan would still have ample scope for his activities. The Hassidic leaders were not without misgivings about the future development of the *Zaddik*. "I can foresee," prophesied the Besht, "that before the advent of the

Messiah, rabbis will sprout forth like the grass of the field. They will delay the redemption because of the division of hearts and causeless hatreds."

There were instances where heredity played no part. Dov Baer of Meseritz succeeded the Besht. Zevi Hirsch Rymanover (d. 1846), a tailor's servant at the rabbi's Court, succeeded his master Rabbi Menachem Mendel. Yet these were exceptions. As a general rule, son followed father almost automatically. Few dynasties became extinct. Inevitably, quarrels occasionally broke out between the various dynasties. To the delight of the Mitnagdim and *Maskilim*, there were unedifying Hassidic controversies that often degenerated into squabbles.

The Besht could not sleep unless all the money in his house had been distributed among the poor. Many of the leading rabbis lived in abject poverty. A great many leaders refused to accept the "gifts of flesh and blood", and had other sources of income. On the other hand, there were *Zaddikim* like the Rizhyner and the Sadagurer who accepted material comforts (*Gadlut Hamore*). They lived in luxury with many servants in their halls and fine horses in their stables. Rabbi David of Talna (Talnoye) sat on a throne of pure gold inscribed with the words: "David, King of Israel." Rabbi Abraham of Trisk possessed a rare *Menora* wrought in silver and gold, which skilled craftsmen had worked years to fashion.

At no time and in no way did Hassidism disparage study. They maintained, however, that Study for the sake of scholarship was a desecration. "A man should study the Torah to become a Torah," was the ideal. Both Rabbi Dov Baer and Rabbi Shneur Zalman were great talmudical scholars in their generation. In the nineteenth and twentieth centuries, many of the Hassidic rabbis in Poland, Galicia and Hungary were acknowledged Princes of the Torah. The Yehudi, Isaac Meir of Ger, Abraham of Sochaczew, Meir Halevi of Ostrowice and Elimelech Shapira of Munkacz were renowned halachic authorities. Many of the Hassidic rabbis in Galicia were styled *Rav*. Among them were the Belzer, the Zanzer, the Shinower and the Bobover.

Contrary to popular belief, not all Hassidic rabbis were "wonder workers". This is another instance of the misrepresentation of Hassidism. Enemies distorted the wonder-working aspect (even though many rebbes—those of Ger, Lubavitch, Kotzk and Pzysha, for example—would have no recourse to miracles at all) and ignored the ennobling influence of the 'Cult of the *Zaddik*', as its detractors called it.

A visit to the Rebbe was a truly religious experience. He was the teacher, counsellor and friend to whom the Hassid could unburden his heart, to whom a Jew in distress could turn at any time for counsel and consolation. The Hassid felt that he had a friend in this world, and an advocate in the world to come. It gave life a new meaning, new colour, new hope. The Court of the rabbi was dominated by the *Gabbai*, who acted as liaison officer between the rabbi and his followers. The Hassid normally presented the rabbi with a *kittel* (petition). "With the grace of God ... A son of B. May he recover from his illness." "May he have children." "May he find a suitable wife." "May he succeed in his studies." A *pidyon* (redemption money) would accompany the *kittel*. The Hassid participated in the *tish* (public meal) with the rabbi. He ordered wine and the rabbi blessed him with : *Lehayyim Tovim Ul'shalom* (a good and peaceful life).

It was also his privilege to secure *shirayim* (remains) of the rabbi's food which were sure to contain the *Nitzotzot* (sparks). *Shalosh Se'udot* (the Third Meal) was the highlight of the Sabbath. The rabbi spoke in illuminating phrases; the Hassidim sang mystical melodies in the gathering dusk; together they swayed and danced in an ecstasy that transcended the barriers of time and space.

The *stiebel* (literally "room") or *klaus* played a vital rôle. It served both as place of worship and as house of study. Hassidic rabbis would establish branch *stieblech* in the various towns where their followers resided. In Poland, most towns had a Gerer, Alexander or Belzer *stiebel*. In the *stiebel* the Hassidim communed with God and with themselves. They discussed the rabbi's discourses and spoke constantly of his sanctity and wisdom.

The *Shivche ha-Besht* was published in Kopys in 1815. Many treasuries of Hassidic fable followed. Hassidim produced legends rather than laws. Great significance was attached to the parable. It was even claimed that there was "no difference between relating stories of *Zaddikim* and the recitation of prayers." Prayer denotes "Praise ye the Lord", and stories are implicit in the phrase: "Praise ye, ye servants of the Lord." (i.e. the *Zaddikim*).

Prayer was the pivotal point of Hassidic life. *Kavana* (devotion) and *hitlahavut* (ardour) were essential for the uninhibited outpouring of the soul. The emotional atmosphere of the *stiebel* was conducive to passionate prayer. The Besht and Rabbi Levi Isaac worshipped with fiery intensity. For Uri, 'the Seraph' of Strelisk, prayer was so devastating an experience that he regularly took the precaution of leaving his 'last will and testament' at home before he left for the synagogue. Yet there were *Zaddikim* (like the Rizhyner and the Sadagurer) who were calm and almost phlegmatic in their worship. "There are *Zaddikim*," it was said, "who serve God with all their limbs and there are *Zaddikim* who fear God so much that they are terrified to move as much as a muscle during the service." Gestures were not regarded as a substitute for true devotion. In the words of Rabbi Nachum of Czarnobyl: "We behold many people engaged in study and prayer ... they raise their voices ... they clap their hands, they jump to their feet. Many ignorant people imagine that this constitutes prayer. The truth is not so. It is fitting that a man should pray in awe and dread."

Whilst drunkenness was abhorred, an occasional drink was permitted, at the conclusion of a service, at the termination (*siyyum*) of a tractate of the Talmud, on the anniversary of the *Zaddik's* death, on Purim and Simchat Torah, at weddings or similar festivities. Hassidim would gulp spirits in careful measure, wish each other "*Lehayyim*" (life), and thus "banish grief from the heart". Asked why the Hassidim drank whisky after the service, whereas the Mitnagdim usually studied a chapter of the Mishna, Rabbi Israel of Rizhyn replied: "The Mitnagdim pray frigidly, without life, enthusiasm or emotion. They appear almost lifeless. After their prayers, they study the Mishna—an appropriate subject when one mourns the dead. But the prayers of the Hassidim are alive and living people need a drink."

The Hassidim followed the established patterns of education. They sent their sons to cheder (religious preparatory school) and to Yeshiva (religious college). Secular objects had no place in the curriculum. "Verily, grammar is useful," admits Rabbi Menachem Mendel of Vitebsk. "That our great ones indulged in the study thereof I also know, but what is to be done since the wicked and the sinful have taken possession of it?" The Mitnagdim and the Hassidim were united in the strenuous and ceaseless battle against *Aufklärung* (known also as *Haskala,* Enlightenment). The solemn warning of the Mitnagid, Rabbi Moses Sofer (1763-1839) of Pressburg, "Touch not the works of Dessau (Mendelssohn)", was strongly underlined by the Hassidic leaders. The Rabbis refused to compromise and erected impregnable defences against the assault of the *Maskilim* and their insidious assimilationist trends. As a result, Hassidism ensured the continuance of traditional Judaism among its adherents and to this day the life of a true Hassid is, to the letter, the life prescribed by Jewish law.

Among the Hassidim, the dance reached the highest level of religious enthusiasm, even to the point of complete self-oblivion. This was no social pastime, no mere 'poetry in motion', no auto-intoxication. This was religious ecstasy, that lifted the participants out of themselves and out of their surroundings, into the highest heaven. The Hassidim danced as they prayed and rejoiced as they danced, fired by religious fervour, *hitlahavut,* not by riotous revelry, by a spirit of awe not by lighthearted gaiety. The dance of the Hassidim was not limited to Shemini Atzeret (the eight day of Succot) and Simchat Torah (the Rejoicing of the Law). They danced on festivals, on the anniversaries of a *Zaddik's* death and on every Sabbath, and the dance was like a prayer, a joyous outpouring of love for the Creator and His Works.

Hassidic music had unique characteristics.[58] Songs

were handed down from Rabbi to disciple and from father to son. They became the "Oral Law" of Hassidism. Every dynasty had its own favourite melodies. These were almost "signature tunes". From the melody a Hassid hummed, it was often possible to identify the school to which he belonged. The tradition of music remained with the Hassidim even to the end, even in the valley of the shadow of death, along the paths that led to the crematoria, where hundreds of thousands of Hassidim perished. It was at that tragic time that Rabbi Azriel David Pastag composed a triumphant melody for the final affirmation of faith. "I believe," he sang and thousands sang with him, "with perfect faith in the coming of the Messiah, and though he tarry, I will wait daily for his coming." This was the faith for which the Hassidim lived and this was the faith for which they gave their lives in sanctification of the Holy Name.

CHAPTER XI

HASSIDISM AND ISRAEL

Throughout their long and bitter exile, the Jewish
people remembered the solemn vow: "If I forget thee,
O Jerusalem, may my right hand forget its cunning.
May my tongue cling to the roof of my mouth, if I do not
remember thee" (Psalm 147. 5). For the Kabbalists, the
land of Israel held a mystical significance. Many passages
in the Zohar express deep love and longing for the Holy
Land. "Happy is he whose lot it is during his lifetime to
abide in the Holy Land. For such a one draws down
the dew from Heaven above upon the earth, and
whoever is attached to the Holy Land in his lifetime be-
comes attached afterwards to a heavenly Holy Land."[54]

Three times the Besht set out for the Holy Land and
every time "Heaven held him back", because it was
known that the fusion of the Holy Man and the Land
would hasten the coming of the Messiah. In vain the
Besht yearned to fulfil the *mitzva* of living in the Land
of Israel. He also wished to plant the seeds of Hassidism
in this hallowed soil. For the Besht did not accept physical frontiers. He wanted his teachings to be known and
studied not only in his native Podolia and Volhynia but
all over the world, wherever there were Jews, and particularly in the sacred cities of Tiberias and Safed. The
Master could not accomplish this task himself but he

tried to accomplish it through others, through his disciples and associates.

In 1743, his brother-in-law, Rabbi Abraham Gershon Kuttower, emigrated to Israel. Rabbi Gershon, a learned Talmudist and Kabbalist, was at one time rabbi in Brody (Galicia). Rabbi Jonathan Eybeschutz spoke of him with the utmost reverence. Rabbi Gershon who had not at first recognised the hidden greatness of his sister's husband, later became a most devoted follower of the Besht. And the Master could ask for no better apostle to carry his message to the land of Israel. Rabbi Gershon was given a warm reception in Hebron and in Jerusalem, where he was greeted with cries of: "Long live the king!" The Besht often wrote to him and even sent him money. In one letter, he counsels: "Rehearse the words of *musar* (ethics) in which I have instructed you many times. Let them always be in your mind.[55] For the Besht, distance was no obstacle to the communion of souls. "One Friday night, during prayers," said the Besht, "I searched for Rabbi Gershon throughout Palestine but could not find him anywhere. On the morrow (the Sabbeth) I found him." Rabbi Gershon explained the enigma. He had spent one Sabbath at Acre in which there were two Synagogues, one inside the town and the other outside the borders of Israel. On Friday night, he had prayed in the synagogue which was technically outside Israel and in the morning he had attended the synagogue which was actually in the Land of Israel.

Rabbi Nachman of Horodenka was possessed of a deep affection for the Besht. He once confessed: "I have afflicted my soul and I have immersed myself in ritual baths but I could not rid myself of alien thoughts till I became attached to the Besht." But Rabbi Nachman's love of Israel was stronger than his love of Rabbi Israel. Together with Rabbi Meir of Przemysl, he settled in the Holy Land during the lifetime of the Master.

The writings of Rabbi Jacob Joseph of Polona are steeped in his longing for *Eretz Yisrael*. "*Eretz Yisrail* is an exalted land. And the Holy One, Blessed be He, hath given it to Israel as a perpetual gift, and it is reserved exclusively and completely for them."[56]Apparently Rabbi Jacob Joseph prepared himself for the pilgrimage to *Eretz Yisrael*. The Besht even gave him a letter to deliver in person to Rabbi Gershon. But Rabbi Jacob Joseph never made the journey and the letter was never delivered. Later, it was published in his book *Porat Joseph*, under the rubric, "This is an epistle which the Besht hath given me to hand over to Rabbi Gershon Kuttower."

According to Rabbi Phineas of Koretz (1726-1791), it was a marked sign of melancholy if a man had no desire to visit the Holy Land. Commenting on Moses' prayer: "Let me go over, I pray Thee and see the good country" (Deut. 3, 25), Rabbi Phineas explains: "Moses said to God: 'I do not wish to emulate the ten spies who brought back an unfavourable and gloomy report. I desire to see only the 'good of *Eretz Yisrael*." In 1792, Rabbi Phineas left Ostrau for Israel but he, too, was unable to complete the journey. He died on the way, at Spitevka, in 1791.

In Iyar 1777, three hundred Hassidim left for the land of Israel under the leadership of Rabbi Menachem Mendel of Vitebsk, Rabbi Abraham of Kalisk and Rabbi Israel Politzker. After a great deal of hardship, they arrived in Israel on Elul 5th. Their enthusiasm knew no bounds. "At last the day has come for which we have waited with such impatience," wrote one of the leaders.

"How happy we are to be in our wonderful land, in the country which is the Holy of Holies."[57] But the arrival of this large number of Hassidim created many problems. Their funds soon petered out and they had no means of supporting their families. "Even a man whose heart is that of a lion melts when he beholds infants begging for bread."

To maintain the Hassidic settlement Rabbi Menachem Mendel enlisted the support of his followers in Russia. He sent Rabbi Israel to raise funds, and Rabbi Israel became the forerunner of many *shiluchim* (emissaries) who paid periodic visits to Hassidic centres in Eastern Europe in order to collect contributions for 'the poor of Israel'. "It is up to you and to us," he writes, "to build up the house of our God and it is for the scattered congregation of Israel to support the settlement of Israel. Great is the *mitzva* of preserving the people who dwell in Israel, of feeding the hungry and clothing the naked, in order that they who live on the holy soil may be enabled to pray for the scattered community of Israel in exile." He succeeded in raising considerable sums but he himself never returned to Israel. As he was passing Pastov, he said: "Abraham the Angel is calling me. He wants me to be buried by his side." Abraham's request was granted.

In many of his epistles, Rabbi Menachem Mendel impresses upon the Hassidim in the Diaspora the importance of the settlement in *Eretz Yisrael*. Even the Sephardim, whose relations with the Ashkenazim were usually rather strained, welcomed and honoured the Hassidic leader. As a result, the gulf between the two factions was bridged for a while and they even intermarried. At a time when fierce war raged between Hassidim and Mitnagdim in Eastern Europe, Rabbi Menachem Mendel and his followers lived in quietude and peace. Rabbi Menachem Mendel's colleagues were greatly impressed by his courage in making the momentous journey and the determination with which he overcame the many obstacles in his path. The fact that Hassidim were living in the Holy Land encouraged others to join them. Moreover, the adoption by the Hassidim of the *Nusach Ari* (Lurian Liturgy) forged another link in the chain of associations that bound the Hassidim with the Holy Land. When Rabbi Hayyim of Krasny (d. 1793) was shipwrecked on the way to Israel, he regarded the incident as a mark of divine displeasure. He left instructions that no titles were to be engraved on his tombstone, because he was not 'worthy enough' to visit Israel.

Rabbi Shneur Zalman, founder of Habad, wished to accompany Rabbi Menachem Mendel to the Holy Land. He could not, however, desert his followers while the Mitnagdim were launching violent offensives, but remained on the battlefield, ready to face imprisonment and persecution. Yet he continued to give active support to the *Yishuv*. He arranged systematic collections and regularly dispatched funds.

Not since Yehuda Halevi (1085-1142) that 'fiery pillar of sweet song', to whom Jerusalem was the 'city of the world', has Zion had so lyrical a lover as the poet of Hassidism, Rabbi Nachman of Bratzlav. The sentiments that Yehuda Halevi expressed in his *Songs of Zion,* Rabbi Nachman voiced in the pithy aphorisms for which he was renowned. Like Yehuda Halevi, he travelled widely in the Holy Land but, unlike the poet, he did not visit Jerusalem. His journeys were minutely described and there are detailed accounts of his visits to Elijah's Cave on Mount Carmel, to the Tomb of Rabbi Simeon bar Yochai at Meron, and to the grave of his grandfather, Rabbi Nachman of Horodenka. Returning home, he could echo the sentiments of Yehuda Halevi: "I am in the west, but my heart is in the East."

Although relatively few of the great Hassidic masters were enabled to make the physical journey to the Holy Land, most of them made the journey in spirit, for again and again they stressed the mystic significance of Zion. Rabbi Levi Isaac of Berdychev loved the land of Israel as dearly as he loved the people of Israel. "When the Jews dwell securely in the Land of Israel," he declared, "then the country is inhabited. But when the Israelites are in exile, then the country is regarded as a wilderness, even though it may be inhabited by other nations. For the Land of Israel belongs to the people of Israel. And only they can inhabit it."

Prophetically, Rabbi Solomon of Lutzk (d. 1813) disciple of the Maggid, saw the future of the land of Israel inextricably linked with the revival of Hebrew as a modern language. In his book, *Divrat Shlomo* (printed in 1859) he declared: "It is essential that the people living there should use the Holy Tongue, the language in which the world was created. If they do not do so, the land does not really belong to them and they can easily be banished."[58]

Throughout the nineteenth century, the links between Hassidism and *Eretz Yisrael* were well maintained. And there were many instances of rabbis giving active expression to their love for the Holy Land. They exchanged comfortable homes for the rigours of a pioneer existence. When Jacob Shimshon, the Sheptever

Rabbi visited his friend Rabbi Wolf Zbaraz in Tiberias, he saw the rabbi's wife labouring over the wash-tub. "Rabbi, this linen is not mine!" she exclaimed, "I am washing it for others, and I am being paid for the task. But I feel no regrets. No sacrifice is too great for the privilege of living in *Eretz Yisrael.*"[59]

Whilst Hassidic rabbis differed among themselves on many problems, they all agreed that it was a sacred and important task to support the poor of the Holy Land. Rabbi Israel of Rizhyn, who was in charge of the *Kolel* of Volhynia and Russia, wished to safeguard the site near the Wailing Wall. He authorised Nisan Beck to buy the plot and to build a synagogue there, the *Tiferet Yisrael* (known nowadays as *Bet Hakenesset Binyamin Beck*).

The publication in 1862 of *Derishat Zion* by Rabbi Zevi Hirsch Kalischer (1795-1874) gave impetus to the *Chibat Zion* (Lovers of Zion) movement. Under the leadership of Leon Pinsker (1831-1891), Moses Leib Lilienblum (1843-1910), and O. L. Lavenda, *Chibat Zion* societies were formed in Russia, Austria and Germany. With the help of Baron Edmond de Rothschild (1845-1934), the first serious attempts at colonisation were made and several settlements were established in the Holy Land. As a rule, Hassidim did not join the movement. Elijah Guttmacher of Krewitz was one of the exceptions. He wholeheartedly supported the work of Kalischer. Rabbi Hayyim of Pilev (1870-1906), son of Rabbi David of Kotzk, went still further. He formed a society known as "*Agudat Ha-Elef*" (The "1000" Group) whose aim was to settle a thousand Hassidim in the Holy Land. Rabbi David was in contact with Rabbi Isaac Jacob Reines (1839-1915) and Rabbi Samuel Mohilever (1824-1898).

His book *Shalom Yerushalayim* evoked the bitter hostility of his fellow Hassidim.

Political Zionism roused the enthusiasm of the Jewish world, but the flying sparks kindled no flames among the Hassidim. The bitter battle still raged between Hassidism and *Haskala*. For, in the eyes of the Hassidim, as we have seen, the *Haskala* movement was synonymous with assimilation and even apostasy. And many of the *Maskilim* carried the flag of Zionism. Moreover, the Zionist solution to the Jewish problem, the restoration of Palestine by political means, was regarded as tantamount to interference with the divine order of things.

Dr. Theodor Herzl, (1860-1904), conscious of the power of Hassidism, was anxious to enlist its active support. In his Diary (May 8th., 1896) he records: "The Hassid Aaron Marcus (1843-1916) of Podgorze (Galicia) writes me a warm letter, in which he holds out the possibility that the three million Hassidim of Poland will give their adherence to my movement. I reply that the co-operation of the orthodox Jews would be highly welcome—but no theocracy will be created."[60] Three years later, in a letter to Rabbi Yehuda Leib Alter of Ger, Herzl earnestly appeals for his co-operation.[61] The Zionist leader kept in touch with Yeduda Menachem Halevi of Przemysl (1862-1920), rabbi in Bostosani (Rumania) who "offered to negotiate with the Wonder-Rabbi David Moses Friedmann (1827-1903) of Czortkow." Similarly, Nachum Sokolow (1861-1936), Zionist and writer, tried to win the sympathy of the Rabbi of Ger. Rabbi Yehuda Leib Alter, however, could not be persuaded. He welcomed the importation of Palestinian *etrogim* (citrons) but opposed indiscriminate immigration. He believed that people who settled in the Holy

131

Land "should be idealists who could be relied on to live according to the laws of the Torah." Among the many rabbis who wholeheartedly supported the use of Palestinian *etrogim* was Rabbi Abraham Bornstein (1839-1910) of Sochaczew. "It is forbidden to use *etrogim* from Corfu when Palestinian *etrogim* are available," he ruled. In 1898, Rabbi Abraham sent his son to buy land in Palestine. But Hassidim on the whole did not share the ideals of political Zionism; they did not work for the realisation of these ideals, and they took no part in the strenuous campaigning that eventually led to the Balfour Declaration (November 2nd., 1917).

On May 27th., 1912, a historical Conference was held at Kattowitz (which then belonged to Germany). Three hundred people attended, a distinguished assembly which included many eminent laymen and celebrated rabbis. Among them were David Hoffmann (1843-1921), principal of the Rabbinical Seminary at Berlin, Isaac Halevy (1847-1914), author of *Dorot HaRishonim,* Hayyim Soloveichik (d. 1920), rabbi of Brest-Litowsk, Rabbi Isaac Hillman (1868-1953) of Glasgow, Dr. Salis Daiches (1880-1945) of Sunderland and Jacob Rosenheim (b. 1871). The outcome was the formation of the *Agudat Yisrael* (Federation of Israel), a worldwide organisation of Orthodox Jews. The aim of the new organisation was "the solution of the contemporary problems of Judaism in the spirit of the Torah."

The *Agudah* aimed also at improving the "economic conditions of the Jewish masses in poverty-stricken countries and in Palestine." And at the First World Conference (*Kenessiya Gedola*) which met in Vienna in August, 1923, it was resolved that the "*Agudat Yisrael* must support the Jewish people spiritually and physically in the Holy Land and abroad." Yet the organisation could never free itself of the anti-Zionist ideas propounded by Isaac Brever (1883-1946): "Zionism will deprive the Jewish people of its uniqueness as upholders of the sovereignty of God."

Between the two world wars of 1914 and 1939, most of the Hassidic rabbis were associated with the work of the *Agudah*. Their attitude to Zionism was negative and they did not co-operate with the Jewish Agency. They believed that "to restore to Palestine Jews without their religion would be to establish the very worst possible form of darkness."

Yet, paradoxically enough, the Hassidim were all passionate lovers of Zion. For most of them, this was a spiritual passion, but there were those who translated the ancient yearning into practical terms. Among them was Ezekiel of Yablona, the pioneering rabbi. He was a descendent of Rabbi Ezekiel of Kuzmir. His own father had once said: "I would rather be a labourer in the Land of Israel than a Rebbe among the Hassidim in the Diaspora." In 1924, with the help and encouragement of Rabbi Isaiah Shapira of Grodzysk and Israel Eliezer Haupstein of Kozienice, Rabbi Ezekiel formed a society called *"Nachlat Ya'acov"* which later became affiliated with *"Avodat Yisrael"*. After a preliminary visit, Rabbi Ezekiel and many of his followers settled in Israel in 1925.

In his autobiography, Dr. Chaim Weitzmann (1873-1952) writes of those early pioneers. "On the way to Nahalal we passed a hill crowded with newly erected barracks round which cloistered a number of people who looked like recently arrived refugees. They made a striking group. We discovered that they were Hassidim who, led by their rabbi (the rabbi of Yablona), had landed in Palestine only a few days before. Many of them had since then been compelled to sleep in the open, which, in spite of the light rains still to be expected in April, they were finding a wonderful experience. Balfour, (Lord Arthur James Balfour, 1848-1930), alighted from the car and went into the barracks to receive the blessings of the rabbi."[62]

The Jewish National Fund allotted them six thousand dunams near Nahalal. At first, there were eighty families. Soon, another thirty families followed. The courage and devotion of the pious workers "aroused general admiration and served to bridge the wide gap that existed between their outlook and that of the workers."[63]

Hassidic rabbis continued to make their way to the Holy Land. Both Rabbi Mendel Alter of Pabianice and Rabbi Abraham Mordecai Alter of Ger visited Palestine several times.

In 1933, the *Agudah* had organized seventy-six *hachshara* camps in Poland with two thousand participants. Their *Keren Hayishuv* Fund collected large sums and the *Agudah* acquired land in Machnei Yisrael, Kfar Saba, Kfar Ita and Herzlia. Rabbi Mordecai Alter, too, in a number of letters urged his followers to support these settlements.

CHAPTER XII

HASSIDISM IN THE TWENTIETH CENTURY

At the end of the nineteenth century, there were six
million Jews in Eastern Europe. They formed a great
and distinguished community; but these 'second class'
citizens were not permitted to pursue their peaceful and
productive ways. A great Jewish exodus from Eastern
Europe began in 1881 and continued with diminishing
tempo until the outbreak of the First World War in 1914.
In all, nearly two million Jews left Eastern Europe; but
relatively few Hassidim were among them. Yet pogroms
were a daily occurrence in the Czarist Empire. The
cries of the victims of Kishinev, "city of slaughter", and
the yells of their persecutors: ("Kill the Jews! Burn
their houses! Spare none!") echoed through a horrified
though unhelpful world. Yet Hassidim hesitated.
They feared the moral dangers of the Godless countries
and the possible effect upon their children even more
than the physical dangers from the murderous mobs.
And their rebbes discouraged precipitous departures
from their familiar habitat.

The Hassidim endured the terror-raids in Russia and
Rumania, the World War, the Russian Revolution of 1917.
"Hundreds of thousands of Jews have been robbed
of their last shirt; hundreds of thousands have been mal-
treated, wounded, humiliated; tens of thousands have

135

been massacred. Thousands of Jewish women become the victims of the bestial instincts of savage hordes. Hundreds of thousands of Jewish women are haunted daily by one idea—that tomorrow they will no longer be able to hold their heads erect. The panic which seized on the Jewish population of these regions is without precedent in all history ... The Jewish masses in the Ukraine are on the verge of madness, and many have actually lost their reason. These unfortunate beings, having lost all that makes life worth living, their nearest, their homes, everything they had, all means of existence, mutilated physically and broken morally, how can they solve the problem of their existence? Where are they to find a shelter? How can they save the children from dying of starvation and cold, and all the accompanying miseries?"[64]

With the Bolshevik revolution and the establishment of the U.S.S.R., the three million Jews in Russia received civic emancipation. But, simultaneously, the authorities instituted drastic and devastating measures designed to extinguish every spark of Jewish religious life. Jewish schools, *chedarim* and Yeshivot were made illegal. Synagogues were requisitioned and converted into workers' clubs. Yiddish was recognised but *yiddishkeit* (Judaism) was outlawed. Yet Rabbi Sholom Dov Baer (1860-1920), the fifth rabbi of the Habad dynasty, remained in the Soviet Union and dedicated himself to the cause of *chinuch* (education). He organised clandestine centres of religious instruction, even in the most remote places, even under the most forbidding circumstances. He sent his emissaries to organise and educate the ten thousand "Mountain Jews" (the "Berg Yidden"), who lived in the Caucasian mountains in the provinces of Grusia and Uzbekistan, and who were almost lost to Judaism.

Rabbi Joseph Isaac Schneerson (1880-1950), son of Rabbi Sholom Dov Baer, was well trained for his task. From the age of fifteen, he had identified himself with his father's manifold activities, and with the help of his brothers Jacob and Lazar Poliakoff he established in Dubrovna, Mogilev, a spinning and weaving factory which became a source of livelihood for many Jewish workers. He even established a Yeshiva in Bukhara. The authorities viewed with disapproval the educational and economic reforms of the sociologist rabbi and he was imprisoned four times between 1902 and 1911. Yet in 1920, when Rabbi Joseph Isaac succeeded his father, he intensified the campaign for Jewish education throughout the length and breadth of Russia. Neither the terror of the Tcheka (secret police), nor the machinations and threats of the Yevsektzia (the Jewish section of the Communist Party), could curb his activities. Forced to leave Rostov-on-Don, he lived for a while in Leningrad.

On Sivan 15th., 1927, he was arrested once more, thrown into the Spalierna prison in Leningrad, and accused of 'counter-revolutionary' activities. He was tortured and sentenced to death, but the sentence was commuted to three years of banishment in Kostroma (the Urals). Through intense political pressure, he was released on Tammuz 12th., 1928 and he settled in Riga, the capital of Latvia. Though he himself had escaped the clutches of the Yevsektzia, the fate of his brethren in Russia tormented him day and night. He travelled to Germany, France, the Land of Israel and the United States of America. Wherever he went, he sought help for the Jewish masses who were dying a spiritual death in the Soviet Union.

Between the two World Wars, Poland was the greatest

reservoir of European Jewry. In 1939, there were three million three hundred thousand Jews in Poland, and they formed nine and a half per cent of the total population. The Jews were the second largest minority and they made up one third of the total urban population. Three hundred thousand Jews lived in Warsaw, one hundred and ninety four thousand in Lodz; fifty five thousand in Vilna; forty four thousand in Lublin, and one hundred thousand in Lemberg. Despite the Liberal Constitution and the Minority Clauses of the Treaty of Versailles, Poland's newly-acquired independence brought neither social security nor religious freedom to the Jewish community. In 1919, the British Government sent Sir Stuart Montagu Samuel (1856-1926), to investigate the position, but his report was ignored. There were provocative municipal ordinances against ritual slaughter, a numerus clausus, Ghetto Benches at Universities, and innumerable economic restrictions that cramped Jewish commerce and poisoned Jewish life.

Leading Polish statesmen openly echoed Nazi sentiments. In 1926, Miedzinsky, Deputy Speaker of the Polish Sejm, declared in the Diet: "Poland has room for fifty thousand Jews. The remaining three million must leave Poland." The "Cold Pogrom" policy was officially endorsed by the State. "My Government," declared General Slawoj-Skladkowski, Premier of Poland, on June 4th., 1936, "considers that nobody in Poland should be injured. An honourable host does not allow anyone to be hurt in his house. Economic warfare is, of course, permitted." But the Polish masses were not content with economic boycott. There were pogroms in Przytsk, Minsk-Mazowieck, Czestochow and Brezesc. After the annexation of Austria by Nazi Germany in 1938,

Poland passed a special law withdrawing Polish citizenship from persons of Jewish faith resident abroad. On all counts, the position of Polish Jewry was desperate. In 1937, more than forty per cent of the Jewish population (including one third of the Jews in Warsaw) applied for Passover relief.

Almost a third of Polish Jewry were Hassidim. Most of them were closely associated with the *Agudah* which obtained majorities in the Jewish communal elections in 1927. The *Agudah* was highly organised, with more than seven hundred branches throughout Poland. It maintained its own network of *Yesodei-HaTorah* (Foundations of the Law) schools, and in the school year 1937-38 nearly fifty thousand boys were enrolled in over four hundred institutions operated by the *Agudah*. The movement published a daily Yiddish newspaper, *Der Yud* (later superseded by the *Yiddische Togblat*), and owned a publishing house, *Yeshurun*. Rabbi Aaron Lewin (1879-1941) of Rzeszow (Reisha) and Rabbi Meir Shapiro (1888-1934) were deputies in the Sejm, while Jacob Trockenheim and Asher Mendelssohn represented the *Agudah* in the Senate.

The prominent leaders of the *Agudah* were all devoted Hassidim of Ger. They included Meshullam Kaminer (1861-1943), editor of the *Yiddische Togblat;* Leib From (1908-1943), co-founder with Yehuda Leib Orleans, of the *Poale Agudat Yisrael*; Leib Minzberg (1887-1943), leader of the Jewish community of Lodz and member of the Sejm; Moshe Deutscher (b. 1880) leader of Cracow Jewry and Moses Lerner (1871-1943) deputy Mayor of the Jewish community of Warsaw.

Among the Hassidic rabbis, there were many remarkable personalities. There was, for example, Rabbi Meir

Yechiel Halevi (1851-1926) of Ostroviec, the "self-made" saint and the ascetic of Hassidism. A man of humble origin, the son of a baker, he became a Hassid of Grodzysk and eventually established his own court in Ostroviec. For fifty years, he fasted by day and ate frugally at night. His writings *Or Torah*, published posthumously, account for his high standing among his contemporaries.

Equally renowned was the dynasty of Biala. The founder was Isaac Jacob, the son of Rabbi Nathan David of Szydlowiec and son-in-law of Rabbi Joshua of Ostrow (d. Sivan 28th. 1873), author of *Toledot Adam*. Isaac Jacob wrote *Divre Bina* on the Pentateuch and in 1873 became rabbi in Biala (Podolska). After his death on Adar II 23rd., 1904, his sons established their own dynasties. Rabbi Abraham Joshua Heschel in Lublin, Meir Shlomo Yehuda in Meseritz (Miedzyrzec), Nathan David in Parczow and Yerachmiel Zevi (1880-1906) in Siedlec. A great Talmudist with rare talents, Rabbi Yerachmiel Zevi was one of the most remarkable of the Hassidic rabbis. When the young Rabbi prayed before the Reader's desk, his melodic voice enthralled the Hassidim. When the young rabbi played the violin, it seemed to the hushed Hassidim that they heard the rustle of wings as the angels themselves gathered round to listen.

Perhaps the most famous rabbi of his generation was the Rabbi of Novominsk, Rabbi Alter Yisrael Shimon Perlow (1873-Tebet 6th., 1933), author of the Haggada *Tiferet Ish,* and many unpublished manuscripts. Scion of the dynasties of Ustila, Koidanov, Lehovitch, Karlin, Apt, Czarnobyl and Berdychev, Rabbi Alter Yisrael Shimon settled in Warsaw in 1917. His home at

10, Franciszkanska became one of the thriving centres of Polish orthodoxy. Hassidim of all 'denominations' flowed to the Novominsker's Court in never-ending streams. The mild and gentle rabbi fulfilled every precept of the Torah with a self-sacrificing saintliness that constantly overtaxed his frail physique. He would speak for ninety minutes at a time and hold his hearers spellbound from beginning to end. His lengthy and learned discourses, his soul-stirring prayers, his mature wisdom spread his fame throughout the country. He knew the whole Mishna by heart and to the end of his life he rehearsed eighteen chapters every day. The Rabbi's brother-in-law was Moses Mordecai Heschel (1866-1918), the Pelcovizna Rabbi. He was the son of the Rabbi of Miedzyboz, Abraham Joshua Heschel and a distinguished descendent of Rizhyn and Apt.

An individualist true to the traditions of Kotzk was the rabbi of Sokolow, Isaac Zelig Morgenstern (1867-1940), who succeeded his father, Hayyim Israel of Pilev in 1894. Rabbi Isaac Zelig first caused a sensation by writing prescriptions in Latin. His concise Hebrew style was characteristically vivid and his brilliant and controversial discourses were the highlight of every *Agudah* Conference. He was a regular contributor to the rabbinic journals *Degel HaTorah* and *Beer*. When Rabbi Isaac Zelig returned from his visit to the Holy Land in 1921, he strongly urged his Hassidim to emigrate immediately. "Go there, for the land of Israel is exceedingly good."

The dynasty of Radzyn was also well known. Rabbi Gershom Heinoch (1839-1891), a grandson of Rabbi Mordecai Joseph of Izbica, was the author of the outstanding works *Orchot Hayyim* and *Sidre Taharot*. He wandered about on the shores of the Mediterranean and became an expert on marine life. He wrote three books on the *P'til Techelet* (the strand of blue in the ritual fringes prescribed by the law of Moses). A workshop for the manufacture of ritual fringes was established at the Rabbi's court in Radzyn and until the beginning of the Second World War the Hassidim of Radzyn and Bratzlav wore a thread of blue in their *tzizit*.

Tens of thousands of Hassidim owed allegiance to Alexander, a dynasty headed by Rabbi Yechiel (1828-1894), Rabbi Yerachmiel Yisrael Isaac (1853-1910), author of *Yismach Yisrael*, Rabbi Samuel Zvi (1910-1924), author of *Tiferet Shmuel* and Rabbi Menachem Dancyger (1880-1943). Just as Warsaw was a stronghold of Ger, so Lodz, the "Manchester of Poland" was the capital of the Alexander Hassidim and Lodz alone had no fewer than thirty five Alexander *Stieblech*. There were few towns in Poland which did not have an Alexander *Stiebel*.

Whilst Ger attracted the scholars, Alexander drew the ordinary *Ba'ale Batim*, the merchants, the masses. There was considerable rivalry, not so much between the leaders of Ger and Alexander as between their followers. Ger reinforced the power of the *Agudah*, while the Rabbis of Alexander stood aloof from political parties. Alexander was the third force in Poland. Alexander associated neither with the *Machzikei Hadat* of Belz nor with the *Agudah* of Ger. Alexander had no place for political machinations, no interest in civic or national elections. The Hassidim of Alexander were left completely free to follow their own political trends. Many of the Alexander Hassidim were closely associated with the work of the Mizrachi (the religious wing of the Zionist Party organised in Vilna in 1902 after the Fifth

Zionist Congress). The main ideal of Alexander was to stress the importance of learning, the significance of congregational prayer and the duty of every Hassid to help his fellow Jew.

The most powerful 'Court' in Poland was that of Ger. The Gerer Rabbi, Abraham Mordecai (1866-1948), was the virtual Emperor of Hassidism and Ger was the capital of his empire. Among his followers were outstanding Rabbinical scholars and leaders of Polish Jewry. The rabbi's influence was far-reaching. A word from him could decide a communal election and any cause honoured by his patronage was assured of success. He identified himself with the policy of the *Agudah* and it was mainly due to his astute leadership that it received the support of the Hassidic rabbis.

When the rabbi of Ger came to town, the visit had the pomp of a state occasion. Mr. (now Judge) Neville Laski gives an eye-witness account: "I heard much talk of the wonder-working rabbis who are almost worshipped by a section of the population. I heard much talk of the wonder-working rabbi of Ger and I managed to obtain ocular demonstration of his popularity; I went to see his arrival from his cure at Karlsbad and was presented with a spectacle such as I have never imagined. Hundreds and hundreds of, to me, mediaeval-looking Jews wearing strange hats and kaftans crowded on the platforms, alongside which steamed a train of the latest type composed of wagon-lits. Excitement reigned supreme. I stood on a railway truck against a fence to obtain a better view, but soon repented, as a surging crowd marching step by step with the rabbi, nearly turned me and my truck into the railway. Four policemen in front, four behind and two on either side, pushed a way through a seething and excited mob, for a very small bent old man who took not the slightest notice of the crowd of admirers who had come specially to see him and went to a motor car, in which he was whisked away, preparatory to his going to his *nachkur*." [65]

The notable Hassidic dynasties of Eastern Europe included those of Kopychinetz, Blasov, Zydachov, Sambor, Sassov, Komarno, Bobov, Parisov, Gostyn, Radoszyce, Rymanov, Dzikov and Strelisk. There were also large Hassidic groups in Hungary, Czechoslovakia, Rumania, Belgium and Austria. The most prominent rabbis outside Poland were the Czortkover Rebbe, Baer Friedmann (1882-1936) and Rabbi Hayyim Eleazar Shapira of Munkacz, son of the great Hassidic scholar Rabbi Hirsch Shapira (d. 1893), author of *Darke T'shuva*. In Munkacz, too, lived the Spinker Rebbe and the Zhidushover (Isaiah Dov Eichenstein).

An important development was the trend towards Hassidic Yeshivot. The rebbes began to establish their own religious colleges and the Hassidic student was spared the difficult choice between inadequate study in the home-like atmosphere of the *Stiebel* and thorough Talmudic grounding in the alien setting of a Lithuanian or Mitnagdic Yeshiva such as Mir, Baranowicz, Radum, Wolozhyn, Telschi, Ponevez and Slobodka.

Rabbi Menachem Mendel Alter Kalisch of Pabianice (near Lodz) established Yeshivat *Darke No'am* and Rabbi Benzion Halberstamm of Bobov (b. 1874) established *Yeshivat Etz Hayyim* with forty six branches throughout Poland. Equally successful was Rabbi Sholom Henoch Rabinowicz (b. 1882) of Radomsk, son of Rabbi Ezekiel, author of *Knesset Yechezkel*. His Yeshiva, *Keter Torah,* opened thirty six branches in

Poland and Galicia. Together with his learned son-in-law, Moses David ha-Kohen Rabinowicz (b. 1900), author of *Zivchei Kohen*, he achieved high standards of learning, particularly at the famous *Keter Torah* colleges at Lodz, Sosnowiec, Bendin, Radomsk, Kielce, Kattowitz, Piotrokov and Czenstochow.

During his residence in Warsaw (1934-1939), Rabbi Joseph Isaac Schneerson founded a number of *Tomchei T'mimim* Yeshivot. Rabbi Samuel Borenstein, author of *Shem Ushmuel*, of Sochaczew, established a Yeshiva under the guidance of Rabbi Arye Zvi Frumer of Koziglov (b. 1880); the great Temple of learning, the magnificent *Yeshivat Chochmei Lublin* (Academy of Learned Men of Lublin) was set up by Rabbi Meir Shapiro (1884-1934) in 1930 and prospered under the spiritual supervision of Rabbi Moses Friedmann (b. 1881) of Boyan.

With the outbreak of the Second World War on September 1st., 1939, the fate of Eastern European Jewry was sealed. The pre-war population of Warsaw was augmented by the transfer of Jews from provincial towns and the influx of refugees from occupied countries. By the time the Ghetto was established on October 16th., 1940, there were between four hundred and fifty and five hundred and fifty thousand Jews. During the three years of agony that followed, there was actually a revival of Hassidism. Many Polish Hassidic rabbis found refuge in Warsaw, and even *Maskilim* would flock to them for comfort in their distress. In the valley of the shadow of death they sang their melodies and spoke their words of spiritual consolation. There was not enough food for *shirayim* to be distributed, but nothing could curb the indomitable optimism of Hassidism.

145

In the *Judenrat*, the Jewish Community Council (at 26 Gzybowsky) set up by the Nazis under the chairmanship of Adam Chernikov, Hassidic leaders were represented. Among them were Isaac Meir Levin, President of the *Agudah* in Poland (later Minister of Social Welfare in Israel), Dov Shapira, Simeon Stockmacher and Eizig Akerman. They all did their utmost to lighten the burden of their brothers. By a decree of the Chairman of the Council of January 20th., 1941, the Sabbath was recognised as an official day of rest. A kitchen for students was opened in Gensha. To the end, Meshullam Kaminer worked on a traditional Yiddish translation of the Bible and Alexander Zusya Friedmann (b. 1897) organised study courses for young and old so that the 'Torah be not forgotten in Israel'.

In the shoe factory of Schultz (44-46 Novolipia) the Hassidic manager, Abraham Handel (now in Tel Aviv) sheltered many rabbis. Among his illustrious workers were Sholom Rabinowicz, son of Rabbi Hayyim Meir of Neustadt; Moses Bezalel Alter, son of the *Sefat Emet*, Abraham Alter, rabbi of Pabienice; David Halberstamm, rabbi of Sosnowiec; Rabbi Kalonymos Shapira of Piasecno, author of *Chovot HaTalmidim*; Alexander Zusya Friedmann and Rabbi Joseph Perlow of Novominsk. A survivor has drawn a vivid picture of this strange factory: "Here you see sitting at the wood blocks and mending shoes (the work mostly consists of pulling out nails with pliers) the Koziglower Rabbi, Rabbi Arye Frumer, the former Rosh Yeshiva (principal) of *Yeshivat Chochmei Lublin* ... From time to time he addresses a word to the rabbi of Piasecno ... *Gemarot* and Biblical texts are quoted and the names of Maimonides, Rabbi Jacob ben Asher are mentioned and who cares now about the S.S. men, about the *volksdeutsch* supervisor or about hunger and misery and persecution and the fear of death! Now they are soaring in higher regions. They are not in the shop at 46 Novolipia Street where they are sitting, but in the lofty halls!"[66]

Some Hassidic leaders, such as Rabbi Moses David Rabinowicz, son-in-law of the Radomsker Rabbi, worked for the *Chesed Shel Emet* (Pinkert) Burial Society. Others were active in *Toz* (the society for the protection of Health among Jews), or the *Judenrat*, which employed five thousand people. The rabbis of Ger, Bobov, Lubavitch, and a few others escaped from Nazi Europe. But most of the Hassidic rabbis in Poland perished with their followers in the action which began on July 22nd, 1942 on the eve of Tisha B'Av. Ringelblum records:[67] "Most of the rabbis were shot during the raids. The long beards and the side locks aroused the hatred of the Germans and many a rabbi paid with his life for his great courage in sticking to his beard and sidelocks." Others were murdered in the Nazi gas chambers, at Oswiecim, Maidanek, Chelmno, Sobibor and Treblinka. Among the martyrs were Isaac Manachem Dancyger of Alexander (Elul 23rd., 1943, Treblinka), Manachem Alter Kalisch (Av 24th., 1942, Treblinka), Moses Friedmann of Boyan (Elul 2nd., 1943, Belsen). Aaron Perlow of Stolin and Jacob Meir Biderman were shot in the streets. Mendel Morgenstern, rabbi of Wengrow, was killed on Yom Kippur.

They died a martyr's death, and they met death with dignity and perfect faith. Hillel Zeitlin (b. 1872), writer on Kabbala and Hassidism, went to his Maker on Elul 10th., 1943, wearing his *tallit* and *tefillin* and reciting passages from the *Zohar*. Of his own accord, Israel

Shapira, the rabbi of Grodzysk, joined a group of Jews who were being taken to the slaughter. "I want to share the fate of my brethren," he exclaimed. To the last moment, he consoled and strengthened them. "I enjoin you not to despair on the way to death," he urged. "Do not refrain from singing the melody: 'I believe with a perfect faith in the Coming of the Messiah' and, like Rabbi Akiva, die with the words: 'The Lord is One' ".

Survivors relate how the frail young Rabbi Joseph Perlow of Novominsk (then thirty years old), wandered around Bergen-Belsen comforting the sick and suffering prisoners. He was so weak that even the Nazis exempted him from work, yet he consistently refused to eat, pressing his meagre ration of bread and water upon others. The eighty two year old Rabbi of Warsaw, Isaac Meir Kanal, deliberately provoked a Nazi by snatching his revolver and he was shot immediately. But he attained his goal, which was, records an eye witness, "to be buried according to the Jewish ritual."[68] Rabbi Heinoch Levin of Bendin offered his portion in the world to come for a glass of water, so that he could recite his last prayers in a state of purity.

Menachem Ziemba of Prague (1882-1942), one of the greatest Hassidic scholars and author of *Zera Avraham* and *Totzaot Hayyim*, together with David Szapira and Samson Stockhammer of the Rabbinical Council, were the spokesmen of *halacha* in the Ghetto. On January 14th., 1943, at the session of the Communal leaders held in Warsaw, Menachem Ziemba declared: "Henceforth we must refuse to wend our way to the Umschlagplatz, which is but a blind and a snare—a veritable stepping-stone on the road to mass annihilation. ... Had we lived up to our presumed status of a 'people endowed with wisdom and understanding' we should have discerned *ab initio* the enemy's plot to destroy us as a whole, root and branch.... As it is now, we have no choice but to resist.... The *halacha* demands that we fight and resist to the very end with unequalled determination and valour for the sake of the sanctification of the Divine Name."[69]

The revolt of the Warsaw Ghetto began on the first night of Passover (April 19th., 1943). On Sabbath afternoon, the fifth day of Passover, Menachem Ziemba was killed by a Nazi crossing Kupieca Street. The streets of Warsaw, Novolipia, Nalewka, Franciszkanska, Mila, Muranowska, once citadels of Hassidism, were now a pile of rubble nearly a square mile in area, physical symbol of the almost total destruction of Hassidism in Europe.

GREAT BRITAIN

At the turn of the twentieth century, London had a Jewish population of some hundred and fifty thousand. Of these, about two-thirds were immigrants from Eastern Europe who had settled in Great Britain during the last two decades. Among the immigrants were a number of Hassidim. They worshipped in the innumerable *Chevrot* they had formed in the East End of London. In 1887, these small congregations were welded by Samuel Montagu, M.P. (first Lord Swaythling, 1882-1911), into the Federation of Synagogues. Among them were 'Cracouer', Fieldgate Street: 'Jerusalem', Union Street: 'Love and Kindness', Prescott Street: 'Great Mile End New Town', Dunk Street: and 'Peace and Truth', Old Castle Street.

A number of Hassidim also participated in the formation in 1896 of the 'Machzike Shomrei Shabbat', later superseded by the 'Machzike Hadat', the Spitalfields Great Synagogue, a spiritual 'fortress in Anglo-Jewry'. In 1896, too, the Austrian Hassidim established one Dzikover *stiebel* at 30, Dunk Street, in the heart of the East End of London and another at 41, Fieldgate Street. Four years later, the Rizhyner Hassidim set up a centre at 13, Buxton Street, and soon after a *stiebel* 'Kehal Hassidim' was founded in Black Lion Yard on a 'non-sectarian' basis, to cater for Hassidim of every type. Among the prominent Hassidim were Asher Weingarten, David Frost (1876-1936), Baruch Wolkovitch (1883-1953) and Selig Oberman (1873-1954).[70]

In the rabbinate, Hassidism was represented in the person of Rabbi Moses Avigdor Chaikin (1852-1928), author of *Sefer Kelalei Haposekim* and *Sefer Tziyyun Rashi*. For thirty seven years (1890-1927), this fervent Hassid of Habad held rabbinical positions in Anglo-Jewry, serving as Minister at Sheffield, as Chief Minister of the Federation of Synagogues and as a member of the London Beth Din.

The Belgian refugees from the First World War founded *stieblech* in Dalston (North-East London) the Schiff Beth Hamidrash (founded by Moses Samuel Schiff) and the Selig Shemien's Shool and a little later, in 1916, Judah (Leibish) Rickel (d. 1929) of Galicia opened a *stiebel* for his countrymen. Among the prominent worshippers were Hayyim David Orlinsky (d. 1941), Hayyim Stark (d. 1952), Hayyim Rothenberg (1878-1941) and Judah Waller (1871-1953), a devoted Hassid of Bobov.

In the 1920s, a number of Hassidic rabbis came to

London; among them were Rabbi Arye Leib Twersky of Trisk (who arrived in 1923), Rabbi Hanoch Heinoch Dov Rubin (d. 1929) of Sassov (who arrived in 1924), Rabbi Sholem Moskovitz of Shatz (1878-1958), Rabbi Israel Arye Margulies (1885-1957) of Przemysl and Rabbi Yehuda Szenfeld (b. 1892) of Kielce.

Most outstanding of the pioneers was a young man of illustrious lineage and remarkable personality. He was Rabbi Nathan David Rabinowicz (1900-1947) of Biala. In 1928, the young rabbi came to London. He brought with him the fire that had inspired the great *Zaddikim* in the golden age of Hassidism. Young Londoners who had never heard of Hassidism flocked to the youthful rabbi and were stimulated by his warmth and sincerity. The rabbi died on Tishri 29th., 1947 at the age of forty seven and his Ethical Will, *Divre David*, was published in three languages.

There are small groups of Hassidim in the North West suburbs of London—in Cricklewood and Golders Green —as well as in Manchester (Kehal Hassidim Synagogue), Leeds (Hassidishe Synagogue, established in 1897), Liverpool (Nusach Ari Synagogue) and other big towns. The greatest number of Hassidim are congregated in North London (in the Stamford Hill area). Cazenove Road, with its countless *stieblech* and bearded rabbis in long *kapotas* and *streimlech*, kerchiefed women (most of them wearing sheitels), Hassidim wearing the traditional garb and youngsters with the long *payot* are a visible reminder of the Hassidic colony in London. Most of the Hassidic Synagogues are affiliated to the Union of Orthodox Hebrew Congregations set up in 1928 by Rabbi Dr. Victor Schonfeld (1880-1930) and extended by his dynamic son, Rabbi Dr. Solomon Schonfeld

(b. 1912). There is to-day full harmony and co-operation between the pious Hassidim of Galicia and Hungary and the Mitnagdim of Frankfurt, heirs of the *Austritt* tradition of Samson Raphael Hirsch. Hassidim play their full part in the work of the Union in *Shechita,* Rabbinate, *Mikvaot, Chevra Kadisha* and *Kashrut.* They operate their own educational network, the Yesodei Hatorah Schools (established in 1943), the Mesifta Talmudical College, and the Beth Jacob Seminary for girls.

UNITED STATES

After the First World War, Hassidic rabbis began to settle in the U.S.A. Among the pioneers were Rabbi Yehuda Arye Perlow and Rabbi Nachum Mordecai Perlow of Novominsk. A dedicated scholar and an active member of the Agudah, Rabbi Nachum Mordecai leads a life of study and service to his devoted Hassidim and carries on in a fitting manner the traditions of his great father Rabbi Alter Yisrael Shimon of Novominsk.

With the influx of European refugees, a small piece of Poland was transplanted to New York. More than five thousand Hassidic families transformed Williamsburg (Brooklyn) into a stronghold of Hassidism. Many Hassidic dynasties are flourishing in New York today. Among them are Satu-Mare (Rabbi Joel Teitelbaum), Boyan (Rabbi Mordecai Shlomo Friedmann), Talner (Rabbi Abraham Twersky), Kozienice (Rabbi Eliezer Simeon Haupstein), Amshinov (Rabbi Yerachmiel Yehuda Meir), Radzyn (Rabbi Yeruchem Leiner), Czarnobyl (Rabbi Israel Jacob Twersky), Blozov (Rabbi Shapira), Kopyczne (Rabbi Abraham Joshua Heschel), Bobov

(Rabbi Solomon Halberstamm). There are also Hassidic rabbis in Chicago, Philadelphia and other cities and States.

Dominating the Hassidic scene is the Habad Movement. Rabbi Joseph Isaac Schneerson arrived in New York in 1940. In the last decade of his life, he threw himself wholeheartedly into a campaign for strengthening Jewish religious education in the New World. He founded in New York the Central Yeshiva *Tomchei T'mimim* with branches in the United States and Canada. He established Bet Rivka and Bet Sarah schools for girls, and formed a Kehot Publication Society which has published and distributed hundreds of thousands of publication, ranging from handbooks on Habad philosophy to elementary guide books on Jewish religion. After the war, the rabbi established the *Ezrat Pleitim Vesidurom*, the Refugee Relief and Rehabilitation Organisation, and to thousands of persons, 'displaced' in body and spirit, he brought material assistance and a message of hope.

The present Rabbi of Lubavitch, Rabbi Menachem Mendel Schneerson (b. Nisan 11th, 1902), son-in-law and cousin of Rabbi Joseph Isaac, studied electrical engineering at the Sorbonne for a time. He has extended the far-reaching and manifold activities of the movement and has accomplished noteworthy work in North Africa. A network of sixty seven *Oholei Yoseph Yitzchak Lubavitch* institutions, evening classes, Bet Sarah and Bet Rivka schools and a Teachers' Seminary have been established to provide for more than four thousand pupils. New Habad brings the teachings of Hassidism to the Sephardim of Casablanca, Marrakesh, Sefrou and Meknes.

153

ISRAEL

Sixty members of the family of the Rabbi of Ger perished in Nazi Europe. Together with his son and his son-in-law, the Rabbi left Warsaw in 1940, a few days before Italy entered the war, and escaped to Israel. His residence in Jerusalem has some of the glory that was Ger. His son Israel has more than ten thousand followers and also maintains a Yeshiva *Sefat Emet* (founded in 1925).

Ahad Ha'am 61, Tel Aviv, was the residence of Rabbi Aaron Rokeach (d. 1957) of Belz. On one occasion, the Jordanians complained to the Armistice Commission of heavy military traffic. It transpired that the alleged 'military convoy' consisted of an escort of two hundred and thirty seven vehicles with Belzer Hassidim accompanying the Rabbi to Jerusalem. During the Sinai campaign (29th., October and November 3rd., 1956) he fasted for three days in a marathon of prayer for an Israel victory.

Notable among the Hassidic settlements is Kfar Habad on the main road from Bet Dagan to Sarfad. This was established in 1949 by Rabbi Joseph Isaac Schneerson as a haven of refuge for the survivors of the death camps. Kfar Habad has its own Talmud Torah and Yeshiva and the farmer-Hassidim breed livestock and poultry. There are also Lubavitch Yeshivot in Tel Aviv, Haifa and Rishon Le-Zion.

Kiryat Vishnitz (Bene Brak) was established by Rabbi Hayyim Meyer Hager of Vishnitz. The settlement has a modern bakery, a diamond polishing plant and industrial workshops and a great Talmudic college *Yeshivat Yisrael Udamesek Eliezer* attended by three hundred students. The Rabbi of Klausenburg, who lost his wife and eleven children under the Nazis, founded Shikun Kiryat Zanz near Nathania, mainly for settlers from the U.S.A. and in December 1959 Rabbi J. J. Halberstam with fifty one of his Hassidim settled in Israel. In 1958, Rabbi Solomon Halberstam founded the townlet of Bobov near Bat Yam.

There are a number of Hassidic rabbis in Jerusalem, Haifa and Jaffa. The most prominent are the Modzitzer (Rabbi Samuel Elijah Taub), the Sadagurer (Rabbi Abraham Jacob Friedmann), the Czortkover (Rabbi Shlomo Friedmann 1894-1958), the Bialer (Rabbi Yechiel Joshua Rabinowicz), the Nadvorner (Rabbi Yechiel Meir Rosenbaum), the Ozarower (Rabbi Moses Yechiel Halevi Epstein), the Rachmastrivker (Rabbi Jochanan Twersky), the Slonimer (Rabbi A. J. Heschel), the Bohusher (Rabbi Isaac Friedmann), the Posganer (Rabbi Moses Leib Friedmann), the Lilover (Rabbi Moses Mordecai Biderman) and the Talner (Rabbi Jochanan Twersky).

The power and scope of Hassidism in the second half of the twentieth century are greatly diminished. There are probably no more than two hundred thousand Hassidim in the world, but this vanishing movement is receiving the ever-increasing attention of writers and thinkers. Martin Buber, creator of a new philosophy, found the mystic Jewish soul in Hassidism. The eighteenth century Hassidic concept of an omnipresent Deity finds support in twentieth century existentialist philosophy. In the wake of Buber, the Legends of the Baal Shem and the Tales of Rabbi Nachman are creating a Neo-Mysticism or Neo-Hassidism. "In a century which was, apart from this, not very productive, religiously obscure Polish and Ukranian Jewry produced the greatest phenomenon we know in the history of the spirit, something which is greater than any solitary genius in art or in the world of thought, a society which lives by its faith." This is the verdict of Buber, author of *I and Thou*.

Hassidism brought new hope and new happiness to hundreds of thousands of people in the darkest days of Jewish history. It brushed away the cobwebs and re-vitalised Judaism not by introducing revolutionary doctrines but simply by leading the people back to the traditional tenets of our faith. It was an enlightened concept, based on the principles preached by the great prophets of Jewry. The radiance that illumined two centuries is dimmed, but Hassidism still has a purpose to serve. Our super-sophisticated over-organised society may recall with nostalgia the soaring ecstasy of Hassidism and the radiance that illumined the Jewish world for two hundred years. And, recalling this, they may well realise that Hassidism has a meaning and a message for the present and the future.

NOTES

1. Dubnow, S. M., *Pinkas ha-Medina* (Berlin, 1925). Halperin, Israel, Actus Congressus (Jerusalem, 1945).
2. Dubnow, *History of the Jews in Russia and Poland,* trans. I. Friedlander (Philadelphia, 1916), vol. I. pp. 116-20.
3. Dubnow, *Toledot HaChassidut* (Tel Aviv, 1930-2), vol. I. p. 14.
4. Pinson, Koppel S. *Nationalism and History* (Philadelphia, 1958), p. 4.
5. Abrahams, I. *Jewish Life in the Middle Ages* (London, 1932), p. 187.
6. *Toledot, Vayyeshev.*
7. *Autobiography* (London, 1954), p. 32.
8. *Ben Porat Yosef, Tsav.*
9. *Shivche haBesht* (Tel Aviv, 1947), pp. 16-18.
10. Horodezky, S. A. *Torat HaKabbala* (Berlin, 1924), p. 15.
11. *Shivche haBesht,* p. 41.
12. *Toledot,* p. 25.
13. Buber, M. *Mamre* (London, 1946), p. 106.
14. Horodezky, *Leaders of Hassidism* (London, 1928), p. 17.
15. Buber, *Tales of Hassidism* (London, 1956), p. 102.
16. Maimon, *op. cit.* p. 154.
17. Minkin, Jacob S. *The Romance of Hassidism* (New York, 1955), pp. 154 and 119.
18. Horodezky, *op. cit.* p. 27.
19. Horodezky, *HaChassidut VeHachassidim* (Berlin, 1922, p. 126.
20. *Ben Porat, Vayyechi.*

21. Finn, Samuel Joseph, *Kirya Neemana* (Vilna, 1915), p. 146.
22. Dubnow, *Toledot HaChassidut*, Vol. I. p. 112.
23. *Testament of the Besht*, p. 23.
24. Dubnow, *Geschichte des Chassidismus* (Berlin, 1931), Vol. I. pp. 181-182.
25. Horodezky, *op. cit.* Vol. II. p. 17.
26. Marcus, Jacob, *The Jew in the Mediaeval World* (Cincinnati, 1938), pp. 276-8.
27. Dubnow, *History of the Jews in Russia and Poland*, Vol. I. pp. 373-4.
28. *Ibid.* p. 376.
29. Steinmann, Eliezer, *Beer HaChassidut, Habad* (Tel Aviv, 1956), Vol. I. p. 231.
30. *Ibid.* p. 231.
31. Horodezky, *Leaders of Hassidism*, p. 49.
32. Teitelbaum, M., *HaRav Mi'Ladi* (Warsaw, 1910), pp. 48-9.
33. Ibid.
34. Dubnow, *History of the Jews in Russia and Poland*, pp. 356-7.
35. Newman, Louis I. *The Hassidic Anthology* (New York, 1944), p. 299.
36. Horodezky, *Leaders of Hassidism*, p. 88.
37. Kitve Rabbi Nachman, ed. Steinmann (Tel Aviv, 1931), p. 305.
38. Steinmann, *op. cit.* pp. 305-8.
39. Levine, Mayer, *The Golden Mountain* (New York, 1931), p. 185.
40. Horodezky, *Leaders of Hassidism*, p. 88.
41. Horodezky, *HaChassidut*, III, p. 31.
42. Steinmann, *Beer HaChassidut*, p. 277.
43. Buber, *op. cit.* p. 273.
44. Bromberg, A. I., *The Rabbi of Rizhyn* (Jerusalem, 1956), p. 59.

NOTES

45. *Ibid*, p. 119.
46. Alfasi, *Einei HaGola*, p. 47, s. 587.
47. Dubnow, II, p. 144.
48. Diaries of Sir Moses and Lady Montefiore (London, 1890), Vol. I. pp. 354-5.
49. Wolf Lucien, *Sir Moses Montefiore* (London, 1884), p. 152.
50. Askenazi, S. *Ha-Isha* (Tel Aviv, 1953), pp. 54-60; Steinmann, *HaMaggid* (Tel Aviv, 1958), pp. 378-390.
51. Jung, Leo, *Jewish Leaders* (New York, 1953), pp. 410-11.
52. Graetz, H. *History of the Jews* (Philadelphia, 1941), Vol. V. p. 375.
53. Zeitlin, H., *Lechassidim Mizmor*, ed. M. S. Geshuri (Jerusalem, 1956), p. 52. Idelsohn, A. Z., *Jewish Music* (New York, 1948), p. 416.
54. *Zohar, Achare Mot*, 72.
55. Heschel, A. J., in H.U.C.A. Vol. XXIII, pp. 20-1.
56. *Porat Yosef, Emor*.
57. Horodezky, *Leaders of Hassidism*, p. 150.
58. Raphael, I. *Sefer HaChassidim* (Tel Aviv, 1955), p. 107.
59. Newman, *op. cit.* p. 302.
60. The Diaries of Theodor Herzl, ed. M. Lowenthal (London, 1958), p. 128.
61. Bromberg, A. J. *Sefat Emet* (Jerusalem, 1957), p. 108.
62. *Trial and Error* (London, 1949), p. 398.
63. Bein, Alex, *The Return to the Soil* (Jerusalem, 1953), p. 378.
64. Elbogen, Ismar, *A Century of Jewish Life* (Philadelphia, 1954), p. 500.
65. Laski, Neville, *Jewish Rights and Jewish Wrongs* (London, 1939), p. 73.
66. Saidman, Hillel, *Togbuch fun Varshaver Ghetto* (Buenos Aires, 1947), p. 142.
67. *Notisn fun Varshaver Ghetto*, by Emanuel Ringelblum (Warsaw, 1952), pp. 297-8.

68. Saidman, *op. cit.* p. 64.
69. Israel Elfenbein in *Guardians of our Heritage*, ed. L. Jung (New York, 1958), pp. 611-12.
70. Oberman, S., *In My Days* (London, 1947), p. 106.

SELECTED BIBLIOGRAPHY

BUBER, Martin, *Die Chassidischen Bücher*, Hellerau, 1928.

DUBNOW, Simon M., *Toledot HaChassidut*, Tel Aviv, 1930/2. *Geschichte des Chassidismus*, 2 Vols. Berlin, 1931: *History of the Jews in Russia and Poland*, trans. I. Friedlander, 3 Vols., Philadelphia, 1916-20.

HORODEZKY, S. A., *Leaders of Hassidism*, London, 1928. *HaChassidut VeHachassidim*, 4 Vols., Berlin, 1922.

LEVIN, Meyer, *The Golden Mountain*, New York, 1932.

MARCUS, A., *Der Chassidismus*, Pleschen, 1901.

MINKIN, Jacob S., *The Romance of Hassidism*, New York, 1955.

SCHECHTER, S., The Chassidim, in *Studies in Judaism*, Vol. I., Philadelphia, 1896, pp. 1-46.

SCHOLEM, Gershon G., *Major Trends in Jewish Mysticism*, New York, 1941.

STEINMANN, Eliezer, *Beer HaChassidut*, Tel Aviv, 1958. *Sha'ar HaChassidut*, Tel Aviv, 1957.

WERFEL, Isaac, *HaChassidut VeEretz Yisrael*, Jerusalem, 1940.

INDEX